MEDIAEVAL SOURCES
IN TRANSLATION

2

ST. THOMAS AQUINAS

ON KINGSHIP
TO THE KING OF CYPRUS

TRANSLATED

by

GERALD B. PHELAN

REVISED WITH INTRODUCTION AND NOTES

I. TH. ESCHMANN, O.P.

PONTIFICAL INSTITUTE OF MEDIAEVAL STUDIES

LIBRARY OF CONGRESS CATALOGUING DATA (Revised)

Thomas Aquinas, *Saint*, 1225?-1274.

  On kingship, to the King of Cyprus, trans. By Gerald B.
Phelan. Rev. with introd. and notes by I. Th. Eschmann.
Toronto, Pontifical Institute of Mediaeval Studies, [c1949].

    (Mediaeval sources in translation ; 2 ISSN 0316-0874)
    xxxix, 119 p.
    Bibliography; p. [108]-115.
    Index: p. [117]-119.
    ISBN 0-88844-251-3

  1. Political science.   2. Kings and rulers–Duties.
I. Phelan, Gerald Bernard, 1892-1965, tr.   II. Eschmann,
Ignatius Karl Theodore, 1898-1968, ed.   III. Pontifical
Institute of Mediaeval Studies.   IV. Title   V. Series.

JC121.T452   320

FOREWORD

The present work is a revision of the translation of St. Thomas Aquinas' *De Regno, Ad Regem Cypri*, which the Reverend G. B. Phelan published in 1935 under the title *On the Governance of Rulers*. The Latin text which formed the basis of Dr. Phelan's translation was that of the current editions and goes back to the Roman edition of A.D. 1570. Comparing this text with a number of authoritative mediaeval manuscripts, I soon found discrepancies not only of a merely paleographical interest but also of "real" importance in regard to the very sense of not a few passages. Hence a minute revision of Dr. Phelan's translation appeared desirable. The Vulgate text of Aquinas' work is scientifically worthless. This fact cannot be overlooked even when only a translation is to be edited. My main efforts, therefore, have been directed towards establishing a genuine Latin text and presenting an English translation which faithfully renders the authentic original. Unfortunately, for technical reasons, this Latin text cannot be published together with the present translation. In an appendix (I), however, I have collected a number of variants which will allow the attentive reader to see the extent of my textual emendations.

The notes to the text are meant to be a contribution to the study of two problems, fundamental for the correct understanding of the doctrine of this treatise. First, the problem of its sources. They have been identified not only when the author gives explicit quotations but also when he tacitly draws from tradition. It is hoped that these findings will help to clear the way for a more accurate study of the wider historical context of the book *On Kingship*. Secondly, care has been taken to show in these notes the immediate Thomistic context of the work, *i.e.*, its relation to Aquinas' other writings. In so doing my purpose was to contribute to the interpretation of the work as well as to the study of the problems of its authenticity and chronology. In Appendix II a selection of the more outstanding of these texts is to be found; only those texts were included which are not accessible in an English translation.

The division into numbered paragraphs is a peculiarity of the present translation, introduced in order to facilitate reference to any part of the work. It is also hoped that this will make it easier to understand the articulation of St. Thomas' thought and argument. The paragraphing has been based on the markings found in the manuscripts, although some liberties have been taken in this regard.

I wish to record my gratitude, first of all, to Dr. Gerald Phelan who generously put his very valuable translation at my disposal. I am also much indebted to the *Pontifical Institute of Mediaeval Studies* whose remarkable collection of photographic manuscript reproductions (the *Gordon Taylor Jr. Microfilm Collection*) made it possible for me to study those precious documents of ancient tradition which are listed in Appendix I. Finally, I wish to express my warmest thanks and appreciation to Dr. Anton C. Pegis, President of the *Pontifical Institute of Mediaeval Studies,* and to the Reverend J. R. O'Donnell, C.S.B., Professor of Paleography, for their most valuable suggestions; furthermore to Mrs. J. N. Holden and Mr. Arthur Gibson for their kind help in preparing my manuscript for the press.

Toronto, March 7th, 1949.   I.T.E.

CONTENTS

CONTENTS

(The titles given to the books and chapters in this table of contents are merely an editorial device. For the chapter-headings found in the manuscripts see Appendix I, *Rubricae in Mss Repertae*, p. 91 ff.)

INTRODUCTION

IN the early Dominican school, two political treatises were composed whose subsequent history was to constitute a curious case of confused identities. The one is St. Thomas Aquinas' *De Regno, Ad Regem Cypri* (*On Kingship, To the King of Cyprus*), the other a work *De Regimine Principum* (*On the Governance of Rulers*) attributed to Aquinas' friend and disciple, TOLOMEO OF LUCCA, who, far advanced in age, died in A.D. 1327.[1]

Both works, such as they are known to-day,[2] were fragments. Although profoundly different in scope and even contradictory in doctrine, they were, within the first quarter of the fourteenth century,[3] welded together by an unknown compiler[4] and, since

---

[1] These two works are most clearly distinguished and called by their proper names in the *Tabula* of Stams; see MEERSSEMAN 59, 64. (The full titles of the works quoted in these notes are given in the bibliographical list on pp. 108 ff).

[2] TOLOMEO's work is only known in the quantity and form in which it is found in the Vulgate editions of St. Thomas' *Opuscula*. Its true *Incipit* has never been ascertained. See below, note 4.

[3] As to the *terminus a quo* of this chronology see B. SCHMEIDLER XXXI f. The *terminus ad quem* is suggested by a remark of JOHN OF COLONNA (c. A.D. 1323): St. Thomas did not, by any means, complete the *De Regimine Regum* (MANDONNET, *Ecrits* 99: *quod quidem opus minime complevit.*) This emphatic *minime* seems to imply that the writer expressed a warning against the apocryphal compound which, consequently, was circulating at the time.

[4] On the authority of a late fourteenth-century MS (O'RAHILLY 408 ff.; GRABMANN, Werke 295), it is often affirmed that TOLOMEO himself was the compiler. Although not lacking a certain probability, this thesis is far from having been convincingly demonstrated. It is also said, on the strength of the same authority, that TOLOMEO composed his *De Regimine Principum* with the intention to "continue" and "complete" St. Thomas' work. On the whole, however, the two writings are so heterogeneous in almost every respect that it is hard to see in them the integral parts of the execution of one design.

then, have frequently appeared in the book market as an indistinguishable literary unit, under one title and one author. As is often the case, the strong eliminated the weak: the new work took on both the powerful name of Thomas Aquinas and the title, extremely popular in the later Middle Ages, of *De Regimine Principum*. A tradition of the genuine Thomistic fragment maintained itself for a while against its bigger and somewhat noisier competitor; it is codified in a number of manuscripts written even after the publication of the *De Regimine Principum*.[5] But its fate was sealed when, in the second half of the Quatrocento, it became an accepted principle with Thomistic editors that, the more voluminous the text they could show, the better. From the age of the incunabula down to the present day, the students of the Angelic Doctor have (with the exception of two obscure fifteenth-century printings[6]) never been gratified with an edition of the genuine *De Regno*. They were always offered the apocryphal compound *De Regimine Principum*.

It is, therefore, not an altogether preposterous statement to say that this genuine *De Regno* is an unknown work of St. Thomas. True, when in the current editions of the *De Regimine Principum* the last sixty-two and a half chapters are cut off, the remainder will prove materially to coincide with the authentic work; which is to say that it is the *De Regno* without any *essential* additions or subtractions.[7] Scissors, however, are not the proper tool to effect a separation of formal nature. In spite of being materially identical, the two texts present certain characteristic differences, which it will be our first task to set forth to the extent to which they may be of interest to the reader of this translation.

---

[5] See the list of MSS *apud* O'RAHILLY 399 ff.

[6] O'RAHILLY 404 f. These incunabula are: Utrecht c. 1473 and Cologne c. 1480.

[7] Several scholars have expressed their doubts about the extent to which the Vulgate text could be held to be in agreement with the authentic *De Regno* — a very reasonable doubt indeed, as long as the details of the latter were still unknown. It can now be stated that no passage of the commonly known text is interpolated. No lacunae are filled in, no parts of the work thrown out of their original place. The fear (or was it rather a hope?) that such might be the case was expressed by MANDONNET, *Bibliogr. thom.* XX, BROWNE 302, and CHENU, *Bull. thom.* 1927, 96.

THE TREATISE *On Kingship* AND THE TREATISE *On the Governance of Rulers.*

These treatises differ, first of all, in their respective titles. Ever since some modern editors of St. Thomas' works, boldly departing from an age-old tradition, refused to employ the title *De Regimine Principum,*[8] the problem of how correctly to designate our work has been discussed in the pertinent literature. Some scholars preferred the title *De Regno* as being more authentic, others chose the title *De Regimine Principum* because it was, and is, more commonly used.[9]

This discussion cannot be expected to lead to any definite result as long as it is conducted in the shadow of that confusion of identities which has always blurred the contours of the literary problems of this work. The correct title of St. Thomas' genuine writing (which is not simply "the first portion" of the work published in the current editions) is *De Regno, Ad Regem Cypri;* and the correct title of the *entire* apocryphal compound is *De Regimine Principum.* In regard to the latter, therefore, the name *De Regno . . .* (used by some modern editors) is just as clearly a misnomer, as is *De Regimine Principum* in regard to the former.

In mediaeval literature, the title *De Regimine Principum* is never used until the end of the thirteenth century, when, replacing the older *Speculum* (Mirror), it appears, from the outset, not as an individual name for an individual book, but as a common name designating that large family of literary productions in which "the man of the study takes upon himself the task of telling the man of affairs what he should do."[10] The primitive history of this title may best be studied with such outstanding specimens of the genre as the pseudo-Aristotelian *Secretum Secretorum* and EGIDIUS ROMANUS' famous work dedicated to PHILIP THE FAIR of France. The former, known at the time of St. Thomas as "Letter to Alexander,"[11] was introduced by the current Latin version as *liber moralium de regimine regum, principum ac dominorum*[12] of which *De*

[8] S.-E. FRETTE XXVII, 336; P. MANDONNET, *Opuscula* I, 312.
[9] See PHELAN 1 f. [10] STEELE IX.
[11] See the references to GUIBERT DE TOURNAI'S *Eruditio Regum et Principum,* STEELE XVIII. [12] STEELE 25.

Regimine Principum is the abbreviation.[13] The latter, a treatise written around A.D. 1280, was presented by the author as *liber de eruditione principum sive de regimine regum,*[14] but circulated from the outset as *Liber De Regimine Principum;* with this title it is designated in the Italian version of A.D. 1288 (*De reggimento de principi*)[15] and in the list of Parisian University books of A.D. 1304.[16] The immense vogue which this work enjoyed right from the time of its first publication was certainly one of the main factors contributing to the popularization of the title. From the turn of the thirteenth century on, it was enough for a work to deal with the ancient topic of the Mirrors of Princes, to be named or also re-named *De Regimine Principum.*[17]

Now, concerning the apocryphal compound *De Regimine Principum,* there is no doubt that throughout its history it was most frequently called by this name. It bears this title not only with full historical right but also as one of its characteristic elements (revealing at once, at least broadly speaking, the time of its composition). It should, therefore, keep this name even in editions or translations which present only a part of it. If, and as long as, the *text* of the *De Regimine Principum* is published, no matter whether in part or as a whole, the editor is, it seems to us, not authorized to change its proper and corresponding title.

St. Thomas' work, on the other hand, was named *De Regno, Ad Regem Cypri* when it was first edited not long after the Master's death which occurred in A.D. 1274. The proof of this is that, clearly, this designation is the one used in the older manuscript tradition.[18] Its authenticity would not admit of any

[13] This title is used, for instance, in the Munich MS *Clm* 14383 (GRABMANN, *Mittelalt. Geistesl.* II, 236.) See also LEHMANN 392, 573.
[14] *fol. num.* 5va.   [15] BERGES 321.
[16] *Chart. Univ. Paris.* II, p. 111.
[17] From the end of the thirteenth century on throughout the later Middle Ages many works *De Regimine Principum* were written (*v.g.* by ENGELBERT OF ADMONT, TOLOMEO OF LUCCA, FRAY FRANCISCO XIMENES, and others.) Other works were re-named *De Regimine Principum, v.g.* PSEUDO-PLUTARCH, *De Institutione Traiani* (BARTOLUS, *De Tyrannia* VIII, fol. 145va), HELINAND OF FROIDMONT, *Flores* (?) (BERGES 295), GUILLAUME PEYRAUT, *De Eruditione Principum* (DONDAINE 165, 221.)
[18] Cf. O'RAHILLY 399 ff.; GRABMANN, *Werke* 294.

objection were it not for the fact that, at an early date, the other title invaded the sources of Thomistic bibliography. The first to have introduced the new name into the nomenclature of Aquinas' writings was, it seems, TOLOMEO OF LUCCA who used it in a list of these writings drawn up perhaps as early as the turn of the thirteenth century.[19] Since TOLOMEO'S authority in these matters was immense throughout the ages, it is not to be wondered at, then, that the tradition of the title De Regno is somewhat inconsistent and erratic in the later Middle Ages.[20] Yet, there is but little doubt, if any, that TOLOMEO was simply using the collective and popular name, the dernier cri in the political literature of his days. A good example of the state of affairs just before St. Thomas' canonization (A.D. 1323) and, at the same time, a confirmation of the view taken here, is offered by the manuscript Vat. Lat. 807, written for Pope JOHN XXII. On fol. 192ra of this Codex we read the following Incipit:

Incipit liber de regimine principum
De rege et regno ad regem cipri

The capital letter D in the second line is very revealing indeed. The rubicator knows that in his days the book is referred to under the title De Regimine Principum which is, to repeat, a collective name. He wants to be up to date and, therefore, composes a first line of his inscription with this "modern" title. Yet he is also faithful to his Exemplar which is manifestly a copy of excellent quality. Thus, after having indulged in an addition of his own making, he returns to the old and traditional title (or rather a trifling variation of it, equally authorized by the older documents).

The compiler of the De Regimine Principum might have had the best of intentions, such as the one attributed to him by a later source, viz., that, dissatisfied with Aquinas' work being a fragment (an intensely mediaeval dissatisfaction), he set out to "complete" it. In fact, however, by destroying, through the change of name, an effective symbol of the identity of the

[19] MANDONNET, Ecrits 62, 56; SCHMEIDLER XXXIII; GRABMANN, Werke 97 ff.—This new title is also found in the manuscript tradition of the authentic De Regno, v.g., in Cod. Lat. 14546 of the Bibliothèque nationale in Paris (XIII-XIV cent.) and in a number of other manuscripts (see O'RAHILLY 399 ff.)
[20] See O'RAHILLY's list and description of the MSS, op. cit. 399 ff.

original, and by dissolving this original into his new composition, he caused considerable damage to the *De Regno.* He made it unrecognizable for fully three hundred years to come. But his damaging interference with the treatise went still further; he meddled, in a most curious way, with the arrangement of the authentic text.

The *De Regno,* according to all authentic manuscripts, contains twenty chapters most frequently[n] distributed over two Books. Not counting the address to the King of Cyprus, Book One extends from ch. I to ch. XII, and Book Two comprises the remaining eight chapters of the fragment. The compiler of the *De Regimine Principum* (a) contracted into one the two chapters XI and XII of the first Book, and (b), set the beginning of a second Book at the original chapter IV of Book Two. At first glance, this might seem to be a trifling matter. But it is not, as will become clear from our later considerations. Suffice it here to observe that the authentic division according to books and chapters (which, of course, was adopted in the present translation) is a very characteristic feature of St. Thomas' *De Regno* as it was set up by its first editor. The main function of this arrangement was to keep in line with the inner organization of the treatise which the author had propounded in the address (§ 1.) Disregarding this and attending only to the proper proportions of his new work, the compiler of the *De Regimine Principum* threw into confusion the original structure of St. Thomas' work. Certain traces of this confusion are still to be observed in recent interpretations and commentaries on our treatise.

It is not our purpose in the context of this Introduction to insist on a number of other details in which the two, only materially identical, treatises differ. We shall turn now to a consideration of the problems of St. Thomas' work itself.

THE CONTENTS AND ORGANIZATION OF THE TREATISE

The story of the book *On Kingship* is not easy to tell. The facts upon which to proceed are few, and they are confusing. When the crust of conjectures is removed, only two facts emerge as historically proven and certain. The *first* is that in

[n] See Appendix I, *Tituli* § 93, p. 91.

the oldest and most reliable sources in Thomistic bibliography the treatise is enumerated among the genuine works of St. Thomas Aquinas, and more precisely among the so-called *Opuscula, i.e.,* the minor works. According to these sources it belongs to Aquinas' writings to the extent to which the reader will find it in the present translation.[22] The *second* fact is that the treatise is unfinished. This incompleteness is revealed not only at the end, where the work breaks off without the author having accomplished his design, but also at several points within the work itself. The *De Regno* presents itself, therefore, as a collection of fragments. Not all its parts are brought to completion, nor is the whole arranged in a consistent order.

It becomes clear, then, that the real problem of this book is to make these two facts consistent one with the other. Nobody will be surprised to learn that not a few interpreters have spent their time playing one off against the other. Those whose first glance fell upon the imposing evidence for the Thomistic authenticity of the work were inclined, if not urged, to dispose in one way or another of its embarrassing intrinsic condition. On the other hand, those who were more impressed by the evidence of the latter devised ways to discount the former. This antagonism is the theme of the long and weary discussions about the *De Regno.*[23] While both disputants were invariably admirers of Aquinas' great and incomparable art of intellectual architecture, one would succeed in finding it, and the other would refuse to recognize it, in the book *On Kingship.* In admiring St. Thomas' power of systematization, the author of this Introduction is in full agreement with both parties, but he differs from some of the disputants in that he proposes to face the facts.

We shall begin with a detailed exposition of the contents and the organization of the work.

In the address to the King of Cyprus (§ 1), the author announces a "book on kingship" which is to contain two parts, the first, on "the origin of kingly government", the second, on "the things which pertain to the office of a king". In other words, one treatise on the theory, and one on the practice, of

[22] On a different *Explicit* of the treatise, which is found in some MSS, see § 130, note 3, p. 73.
[23] See FLORI 5-46.

royal power were planned. The subject-matter which is indicated by the words "the origin of kingly government" does not promise an historical investigation. Rather, according to mediaeval terminology,[24] it states the problem of the rational "origin" of monarchy, *i.e.,* its foundation in rational principles. St. Thomas' intention is to answer the question: Why is it that one man, *i.e.,* a monarch, should in a given society be set over all other men?—a specification and development of the famous problem:[25] Why is it that man is set over other men?

How is this program followed out in the treatise?[26] The initial words of II, 1 (§ 93) show that the practical part starts at this point. The manuscript tradition of the authentic portion of the work is therefore correct in starting a new book at § 93. Now, since the dichotomy in the prologue is formal and exhaustive, Book One, *i.e.,* the part preceding § 93, will rightly be expected to contain the theory of kingship, and nothing but that theory. In fact, however, Book One contains much more. To the theory of monarchy a large treatise is added which patently has nothing to do with it, *viz.,* chapters 7 to 12 (§§ 53-92). In these chapters St. Thomas presents an elaborate tract (in point of form the most perfect part of the work) on the reward of a king who performs his duty well and, correspondingly, on the punishment of a tyrant who fails to do so. The rubricator of the manuscript Toledo, Chapter Library, 19-15, calls this tract a treatise *On the Reward of a King* and, by introducing a new numbering of the chapters, treats it as an independent unit. After numbering ch. 7 as *capitulum primum* (fol. 80vb) and ch. 8 as *capitulum secundum* (fol. 81rb) of a treatise *De Praemio Regis,* he (or his predecessor) apparently looses the courage to stand by this unusual, though not at all preposterous, idea. Whatever was his reason, the treatise *On the Reward of a King* is clearly out of place. It belongs not to the theoretical but to the practical part of the work. True, the text takes care, in § 53, to make a positive connection with the foregoing part: "Since, according to what has been said so far, it is the king's duty to seek the good of the multitude . . . ," but in §§ 13 and 15 this

---

[24] See JOHN OF PARIS, *De Potestate Regia et Papali,* ed. LECLERCQ 176 f.
[25] CARLYLE I,.113 ff. 125 ff. St. Thomas, *Summa* I, 96, 4.
[26] On what follows *cf.* BROWNE 300 ff.

intention of the common good was treated in a theoretical, not
yet a practical fashion; it was presented as part of the definition of a king, not yet, formally, as the constitutive principle
of his office. It is true again that in the epilogue (§ 92) the
tract *De Praemio Regis* is explicitly affirmed to be an integral
part of Book One. Nevertheless, the contradiction between
the scheme of § 92 and that of § 1 is neither mentioned nor
explained, and there is no way of adopting both schemes
together.

It is interesting to observe the attitude of commentators in
the face of this contradiction. Nobody, to my knowledge, denies
it explicitly, but many, choosing the old and not altogether
unwise tactic of the ostrich, simply do not mention it. Others,
facing it, grasp at the most fantastic explanations, for instance,
that the *De Regno* is an incompetent report, by one of Aquinas'
disciples, of the Master's lectures.[27] Still others minimize the
difficulty by saying that we should not expect this work to be
an "organic doctrinal treatise constructed in accordance with
the rigorous laws of logic", but that it should be taken rather
as a "pedagogical tract" in which "it was only natural for St.
Thomas to abandon his speculative and rational consideration
[I, 1-6] and slip into an exhortative sermon [I, 7 ff.]".[28] If
the question is what was "only natural for St. Thomas", it
would seem that this was to do the right thing in the right
place. Nor is it of any avail with BERNARD DE RUBEIS[29] and
CHARLES JOURDAIN[30] to point to an intrinsic and abstract con-
tinuity of the parts I, 1-6 and I, 7-12, which of course it is
easy to bring under a common denominator. In recent times,
CHARLES JOURNET[31] and W. BERGES[32] follow this same line of
interpretation, based exclusively on § 92. The former suggests
grouping these parts under the heading: *The advantages of
monarchy,* and subdividing thus: (a) . . . *for the multitude*
(chapters 2-6); (b) *for the king* (chapters 7-12). The latter
proposes to see in part (a) a treatise dealing with the meaning of the institution of monarchy (*ratio regiminis*), while part
(b) would appear as a treatise revealing to the king the

[27] GIUSEPPE CARLE, *La vita del diritto ne' suoi rapporti con la vita
sociale* (Torino, 1890) 231; quoted by FLORI 32.
[28] ROGUET VII. [29] *Diss.* XXII, 2: CCLV. [30] *La phil. de s. Th.* I, 147.
[31] *Préface* XVIII. [32] *Fürstenspiegel* 204, n. 4.

meaning of his personal life (*ratio regis*). Some such principle
of division is indeed perceptible in § 92, but the real problem
is the compatibility of either part with the scheme announced
in the address.

The treatise on the reward of a king is thus a fragment in
this sense that, although complete in itself, it is nevertheless
a piece that is out of place. An attentive analysis of the *De
Regno* easily reveals more fragments of the same kind, as well
as fragments of a different sort, *viz.*, pieces that are incomplete
in themselves.

Consider the treatise on monarchy (I, 2-6), which is obviously a development of the topic announced in the address,
viz., the "origin" of kingship (*i.e.*, its derivation from rational
principles). The construction of this treatise is clear and
simple. The author starts with a consideration of the absolute
merits of monarchy (I, 2 and 3), moves on to a remarkable
discussion of its historical merits (I, 4 and 5), and announces
at the beginning of ch. 6 (§§ 41-42) a third part dealing with
the conditions under which monarchy may flourish with the
minimum of danger of degenerating into tyranny. This
announcement, according to a rule followed throughout the
work, clearly intends to assign to ch. 6 its topic, and the
sentence at the end of § 42 ("How these things may be done
we must consider in what follows") points to what was to be
elaborated at once, not in some other more distant part of the
work, for these conditions belong to the theory of monarchy
as envisaged by the author. Yet the development of this
point is lacking. Instead, with a telling "Finally" (*demum*,
§ 43), the treatise jumps to another question, *viz.*, what is to
be done if all the limits put on the constitution and the
exercise of royal power should fail to produce their effect.
Only on this supposition does it make sense, in the context, to
discuss the problem of resisting a tyrant. St. Thomas deals
with it in the fragment extending from § 42-52, a fragment
complete in itself but lacking its proper connection with the
context. This famous passage might have concluded the first
and theoretical part of the work. As it stands, this part
consists of two fragments, the one extending over §§ 16-42, the
other over §§ 43-52.

A similar case of rupture can be observed in the Second
Book between §§ 102 and 103 (II, 3 = I, 14). At the beginning
of the Second Book, the principle of its method and construction is laid down, viz., that the right practice of royal government is to be discovered by studying the model of God's
government of the universe (93-95). Faithful to this method,
the author deals with the foundation of a kingdom which is
considered to be the first part of the kingly office, just as
God's first work in regard to the world is its creation (96-101).
In § 102 he proceeds, in perfect conformity with the established
plan, to announce the topic of the chapter to follow: "Just as
the founding of a city or kingdom may suitably be learned
from the way in which the world is created, so too the way
to govern may be learned from the divine government of the
world". However, this announcement is all there is to the
chapter. What follows in §§ 103-122 is a lesson in governmental practice drawn, not from the theological teaching on
God's providence, but from the ecclesiastico-political teaching
on the relations between the two powers. It is not a treatise
on how a king should govern by learning from the divine
model, but how a king in Christendom should govern by
being subjected in spiritual matters to the "divine government
administered by the priest" (§ 114). As they stand, these are
two unconnected topics. A way could have been found to
make one continuous with the other. Innocent III, for example,
in the famous Caput Solitae Benignitatis,[33] had deduced the
ecclesiastico-political doctrine from the fact that God governs
the physical world "by the two great lights in the firmament,"
symbols of Church and State. Or, if this symbolic exegesis
is perhaps extraneous to Aquinas' mind, we might suppose
the link to have been some such considerations as are presented in Contra Gentiles III, 78 (cf. ibid., 83). But any such
link is missing here where the matter of the divine government of the world gets only a plainly incidental mention in
§ 120. So there are again two fragments, the one on the
analogy of divine and human government (93-102) being a
piece broken off at the end, and the other, on the office of a
king in Christendom (103-122) being complete in itself but
left without explicit integration into the whole.

[33] Decretales Gregorii IX, L. I, 33, 6: FRIEDBERG 198.

The first chapter of Book I contains "preliminary remarks," according to the statements in §§ 2 and 16. Before explaining his theory of kingship the author exposes what is meant by the word *king*. Instead, however, of setting forth this meaning in a simple fashion (as John of Paris does in a résumé of *De Regno* I, 1 and 2, in the first chapter of a political pamphlet written in A.D. 1302),[34] St. Thomas chooses to begin at the beginning, *i.e.*, at the natural fact of human society (§§ 3-7). He then establishes the necessity of some governing power, whichever it may be, in every human society (§§ 8-9), and only thereafter, through an eliminative procedure based on an Aristotelian division of the specific forms of government, arrives at his notion of a king. The road which the reader is led to travel is thus not an easy one. In fact, its many turns, together with the structural obscurities of the whole work, have caused not a few mistakes of interpretation. The rubricators of the partly spurious four books *De Regimine Principum* completely failed to recognize the significance of this chapter and, over-emphasizing one point of its teaching, couched the chapter-heading thus: "Men, living together, must be diligently ruled by somebody."[35] Recent interpreters look upon this chapter as a treatise on the origin of kingship.[36] This is an inaccurate view, if for no other reason than that no author treats a principal part of his program in a passage in which he sets forth "preliminary" remarks. Moreover, the origin of that specific form of government which is kingship is not even mentioned in this chapter. What is mentioned is the rational origin of government in general, and this is done in the course of an argument intended to bring out the definition of monarchy, which the author wants to be understood as a preparatory step to his main discourse. The following chapter-heading, therefore, which is found in some manuscripts,[37] is the only correct one: What is meant by the term "king"? The first chapter of Book I is, apart from the address to the King of Cyprus, the only unbroken and well-integrated piece of the work.

[34] *De Potestate Regia et Papali*, ed. Leclercq 176 ff.
[35] *Quod necesse est homines simul viventes ab aliquo diligenter regi*, Vat. Lat. 810, fol. 1va.
[36] Ch. Journet XVIII.   [37] See Appendix I, *Tituli* § 2, p. 91.

In the following chart, we have tried to present the contents and organization of the *De Regno,* and at the same time to mark out the fact that the work is but a collection of fragments.

The address to the King of Cyprus		§ 1
Preliminary remarks: on the meaning of the term *monarch*		ch. 1
First Book: The theory of monarchy — The theory of monarchy	Its absolute merits	ch. 2, 3
	Its historical merits	ch. 4, 5
	Limited monarchy	ch. 6 (41, 42)
	The problem of resisting a tyrant	ch. 6 (43-52)
	The reward of a good king	ch. 7-11 (53-90)
	Epilogue of the First Book	ch. 12 (91, 92)
Second Book: the practice of a monarch — The king's duties in general	The analogy of divine and human government	ch. 1-3 (93-102)
	The monarch in Christendom	ch. 3-4 (103-122)
	The king's duties in particular: in regard to the foundation of a kingdom	ch. 5-8

The problem of the authenticity

Is the *De Regno* an authentic work of St. Thomas Aquinas? The answer to this much debated question is: Yes, it is. The demonstration of this Thomistic authenticity is very imposing indeed. It was first set forth by the great JACQUES ECHARD, O. P., in the monumental synthesis of Dominican bibliography, *Scriptores Ordinis Praedicatorum*[38] (A.D. 1719). He founded it on the two outstanding sources in Thomistic bibliography, *viz.*, the manuscripts and the so-called Catalogues, *i.e.*, lists of Aquinas' writings drawn up for biographical and bibliographical purposes by competent and conscientious experts, not long after St. Thomas' death. ECHARD's demonstration, conducted as it was with an admirable method, is still valid to-day. Only its material basis has been greatly enlarged and solidified. Manuscript research undertaken by MARTIN GRABMANN[39] and especially ALFRED O'RAHILLY,[40] has brought to light twenty-seven manuscripts, most of them presenting the twenty chapters of the *De Regno* and definitely ascribing this work to St. Thomas. On the other hand, the studies of HEINRICH DENIFLE,[41] PIERRE MANDONNET,[42] P. SYNAVE,[43] MARTIN GRABMANN,[44] G. MEERSSEMAN,[45] H.-D. SIMONIN,[46] and others, have considerably advanced our knowledge of the Catalogues. To the ordinary reader of this treatise it will be of no interest to know all the details of this demonstration. One detail, however, should be carefully considered and pondered.

In mediaeval literature, the *De Regno* appears for the first time only after St. Thomas' death. In its first edition it is part of a volume containing Aquinas' *Opuscula*, or, as it were, his Collected Papers. These papers were partly posthumous writ-

[38] I, 336 f.   [39] *Werke* 132-240.
[40] *Irish Eccl. Rec.* XXXI, 398-410. To the twenty-five MSS listed by O'RAHILLY (cf. *ibid.* 614) two more are to be added, viz., Bologna, *Bibl. Univ.* 861 (1655) and Basel, *Universitätsbibl.* B. VII (GRABMANN, *Werke* 296, F. PELSTER, *Scholastik* IV, 129.) No information is so far available concerning the apocryphal text and its history.
[41] *Archiv f. Literatur- u. Kirchengesch.* II, 165-248.
[42] *Des écrits authentiques de s. Th.;* ed. *Opuscula, Introduction.*
[43] *Archives d'hist. doctr. et litt.* III, 25-103.   [44] *Werke* 53-132.
[45] *Monum. Ord. Fr. Praed. Hist.* XVIII.
[46] *Archiv. Fr. Praed.* VIII, 193-214; IX, 192-213.

ings (such as the *De Regno*) and partly re-editions of works already existing in separate publications put out by St. Thomas himself, but fitting the notion of *Opuscula* (minor works) which the new editor intended to collect. Neither the name of this editor nor the exact date of his edition are known, but it is probable, though far from certain, that the collection originated shortly after St. Thomas' death and that REGINALD OF PIPERNO, the Master's secretary of long standing and proven competence, had a hand in it. If it is true that EGIDIUS ROMANUS' *De Regimine Principum* supposes St. Thomas' work to have been known,[47] we might conclude that this collection of *Opuscula* was made within five or six years after Aquinas' death—a date which P. SYNAVE, on the basis of other observations, also believed to be probable.[48] In any case, it is of primary importance in regard to the present problem of authenticity to insist on the fact that neither the collection as a whole nor the *De Regno* are known before 1274. St. Thomas, therefore, never edited this work. He never handed over his manuscript, or dictated the text, to a qualified scribe writing the apograph, *i.e.*, the first copy, which was, as a rule, corrected and authorized by the author, and used thereafter as the source of further transcriptions. Nor did St. Thomas, for reasons unknown to us, cause a fair copy of this work to be sent to its addressee, the King of Cyprus. If the date of its composition is to be set in the first half of the sixties, as shall be shown later, we obtain about fifteen years during which no trace of the work can be ascertained. Thereafter, it was published without the support and approval of its author.

What follows from this fact of an authenticity lacking the author's authentication? Let us carefully note, in the first place, that in and by themselves the peculiar circumstances of the edition constitute no sufficient reason to shake the presumption, based upon the prima-facie evidence of external criticism, of St. Thomas' full and unrestricted authorship. In regard to these circumstances the *De Regno* is no worse off than many other works, for instance, the *Tertia Pars* of the *Summa,* or, to give an example within the *Opuscula* themselves,

---

[47] GRABMANN, *Studien* 67; MARIANI, *Scrittori politici* 135.
[48] *Loc. cit.* 92.

the *Compendium Theologiae,* for neither work was edited by Aquinas. From the point of view of the available extrinsic evidence, the authenticity of the *De Regno,* as MARTIN GRABMANN correctly stated, is just as good as that of the *Compendium.* It would be entirely unjustifiable to cast even a slight suspicion upon the editor of the *Opuscula* that he might have smuggled into the collection a book of his own or alien make. On the other hand, if we consider the circumstances of the edition together with the intrinsic condition of the text, they at once appear in their proper import. In no way do they contradict the following hypothesis which is strongly suggested by the intrinsic analysis of the text; on the contrary, they leave room for such an explanation. After all, the shape and organization in which we find the text of the *De Regno* are not nearly as good as those of the *Compendium Theologiae.*

Our hypothesis, then, is this: there is reason to think that St. Thomas' autograph of the *De Regno,* although lacking the author's last finishing touch, contained a complete work. It is the presence, in our actual copy, of the treatise on the reward of a king which seems to justify this assumption. This treatise is manifestly a peroration whose natural place is therefore at the very end of the work. St. Thomas, however, was too capable and experienced a writer to compose a peroration without having completed the main part of his discourse. Moreover, it is hard to believe that Aquinas himself would have left parts of his work in as fragmentary a state as they are found now. This would imply a tentative and provisional way of writing which is incompatible with St. Thomas' known practice. If, however, it is true that in the original manuscript the work was complete, some accident must be assumed to have happened to it during the long years after it was abandoned, for reasons unknown to us, by the author. Perhaps it was kept by his secretary who either carried it around with him on extensive journeys through Italy to Paris, and back again to Naples, or left it in the custody of some Dominican convent. At any rate, some sheets of the manuscript were lost and its parts disarranged. When, therefore, the editor (*i.e.,* the writer of the first apograph) found the treatise among St. Thomas' posthumous papers, he held in his hands a disarranged collection of fragments. Had he been a modern editor, he would have taken the utmost care to describe the exact condition in which he had found these papers. But being a mediaeval man, his very first concern was to present to his prospective readers a work as complete as possible. The mediaeval horror of a literary vacuum which prompted some later editor to tack on to the Thomistic treatise a long work thoroughly different in style and character—this *horror vacui* was to a limited extent already at work in the first editor. He seems to have taken the liberty to round out the edges of the different pieces and to make the fragments fit together, thus giving the work what he thought to be a presentable fullness of form. He probably did not alter it very radically. The fragments in themselves, we believe, are what was left of St. Thomas' work. Some connecting words or phrases, however, may be ascribed to this first editor; and we are especially thinking of some words at the beginning of §§ 43 and 103, and of the epilogue in I, 12, particularly of § 92. These and a few other obvious incongruities[40] do seem to betray another hand than that of St. Thomas.

To resume and exactly formulate this opinion: the *De Regno* is made up of genuine Thomistic fragments and is thus in its material substance an authentic work of St. Thomas. Its formal unity is also authentic to the extent to which the organization outlined in the address is still preserved in the present treatise. Where this is not the case, the resulting disarrangement must be attributed to the first apograph. — There is no need to stress the hypothetical nature of this opinion. Yet, it has two advantages. First, it takes account of all the facts, which must be and remain the essential elements of our judgment. Second, it effects a concordance of the two

[40] See I, 1, note 18, p. 8; I, 3, nn. 9-11, p. 16-17. The frequent occurrence of plagiarism, especially in regard to the quotations from the Aristotelian Politics, is also a somewhat puzzling feature of this work.—The autograph was probably written in Aquinas' so-called undecipherable handwriting of which the reader may see some speciments in the Leonine edition of the *Contra Gentiles*. If we supposed this first editor to have been a less competent reader of this *littera inintelligibilis*, the explanation of some difficult passages would perhaps be easier. Inexperienced editorship is not infrequently noticeable in the first editions of St. Thomas' posthumous works.

methods of criticism —extrinsic and intrinsic—which, especially as they have been handled in the case of this book, have often appeared to be irreconcilable.

THE CHRONOLOGICAL PROBLEM

No direct and reliable extrinsic evidence is available for the year in which St. Thomas composed this work. Its chronology is so shrouded in mystery that MARTIN GRABMANN, after relating the attempts made hitherto to penetrate it, concludes: The chronology of the *De Regno* will never be known with certainty.[50] The usual method of attacking this problem has been to identify the King of Cyprus to whom the work was dedicated. There are three eligible candidates: HENRY I OF LUSIGNAN (1218-1253), HUGH II OF LUSIGNAN (1253-1267) and HUGH III OF ANTIOCH-LUSIGNAN (1267-1284). Each has been selected by one scholar or another for the honour of being the "Royal Highness" mentioned in the first lines of the *De Regno*.

When P. A. UCCELLI discovered the *Codex Vaticanus Latinus* 5088 with its beginning: *Incipit liber fratis thomaxii ad henricum regem cypri,* he was happy to proclaim HENRY I as the addressee.[51] Yet this attribution is clearly impossible since the *De Regno* is full of quotations from Aristotle's Politics, and this Aristotelian book was certainly unknown to St. Thomas up to 1259 or 1260. The identification made in *Vat. Lat.* 5088 is probably nothing but an inconsiderable statement of the rubicator, who had in mind HENRY II (1285-1324), the king who achieved a bad reputation, probably undeserved, through being chastized by DANTE[52] as "Famagusta's and Nicosia's [the two main Cypriote cities] beast who keepeth even footing with the rest" (of blameworthy kings).

The Dominican STEPHEN OF LUSIGNAN is the only voice from Cyprus ever to mention a name in this matter. In a work published in 1573 his identification falls upon HUGH III,[53] "The

---

[50] *Werke* 297.   [51] *Intorno a' due opuscoli* 10.
[52] *Paradiso* XIX, 147 f.
[53] *Chorograffia et breve historia universale dell' isola de Cipro* . . . Bologna, 1573, f. 54 b; *Histoire contenant une sommaire description des genealogies* . . . *de tous les Princes* . . . *qui ont iadis comma(n)dé ès Royaumes de Hierusalem, Cypre* etc. Paris, 1579, f. 17 b: both works quoted by HILL 157, n. 4. See also *Script. O. P.* 337.

Great" as he is called in Cypriote documents, having recovered
for himself and his successors the coveted title "King of
Jerusalem" which had belonged to the founder of the Cypriote
Lusignan dynasty. Since STEPHEN was not only a native of
Nicosia but a scion of the royal family to one of whose members
the dedication of the *De Regno* certainly applies, it might be
surmised that he drew his information from a family tradition
or from a tradition of the Cypriote Dominicans. Relying on
this authority, surely of no negligible weight although not
absolutely convincing, modern historians such as CHARLES
JOURDAIN,[54] WILLIAM STUBBS[55] and RENE GROUSSET,[56] refer St.
Thomas' work to HUGH III.

JACQUES ECHARD, the most prominent of the older Thomistic
bibliographers, disagrees with STEPHEN OF LUSIGNAN. He points
out[57] that St. Thomas, whose family were subjects of CHARLES
D'ANJOU, would hardly have sought the patronage of HUGH
III whom the Angevin considered as his rival in the struggle
for the crown of Jerusalem.[58] Moreover, he draws attention to
the fact that HUGH II was a boy during his reign (he died at the
age of fifteen), while his cousin HUGH III was a man of mature
age when he came to power. Would not the pedagogical tenor
of Aquinas' book, which it shares with all mediaeval "Mirrors
of Princes" better fit the younger man? ECHARD is followed in
this opinion by BERNARD DE RUBEIS,[59] PIERRE MANDONNET,[60] and
also by historians of Cyprus such as LOUIS DE MAS LATRIE[61] and
GEORGE HILL.[62]

Whatever be the value of ECHARD's conclusion in itself, his
arguments are not much convincing. CHARLES D'ANJOU's claim
to the crown of Jerusalem hardly became public before A.D.
1277,[63] *i.e.*, three years after St. Thomas' death, when MARY OF

---

[54] *Op. cit.* I, 148.   [55] *Seventeen Lectures* 204.
[56] *Hist. de l'Orient latin* 512.   [57] *Script. O. P.* I, 337.
[58] During the pontificate of CLEMENT IV, the Dominican superiors,
especially those of the *Provincia Romana* (to which St. Thomas belonged), had to impose silence on those of their subjects who criticised
CHARLES' political deeds; WALZ 121. On the relations between St. Thomas
and the Angevin in the years 1272/3 see WALZ 175.
[59] *Diss.* XXII, 1: CCLIV.   [60] *Introduction* LII.
[61] *Hist. de l'Ile de Chypre* I, 419.   [62] *A History of Cyprus* II, 157.
[63] Before A.D. 1272 CHARLES had addressed HUGH III as king of
Jerusalem. Only in 1272 did he find reasons to modify his attitude and
to support MARY OF ANTIOCH's claim. In 1277 the contract between
MARY and CHARLES was signed: HILL 163 f.

ANTIOCH, another claimant, sold whatever rights she might have had to the Napoleon of the thirteenth century. Further, it is not correct to regard the Mirrors of Princes, and more especially St. Thomas' work, as pedagogical treatises, in the strict sense of the word. Sometimes they were such, like VINCENT OF BEAUVAIS' *De Eruditione Filiorum Regalium*,[64] but often they were not. St. Thomas' Mirror, at any rate, is of the same general character as the *Eruditio Regum et Principum* which ST. LOUIS OF FRANCE, at the height of his maturity as man and king (A.D. 1259), had requested of the Franciscan GUIBERT OF TOURNAI, for his own guidance and meditation.[65] Yet, in spite of his inconclusive reasoning, ECHARD'S statement can be shown to be correct in itself, by employing another method of investigation, a method which, again, admits the text of the *De Regno* as evidence. Why indeed should this text be kept out of the discussion?

There are several points in the teaching contained in the *De Regno* which would make it difficult to fit it into the context of St. Thomas' works, if it is supposed that it was written after 1267, *i.e.*, after the death of HUGH II, which occurred on December 5th of that year. These difficulties will appear clearly if a comparative study, extending over the corresponding passages in different Thomistic works, is made of the following two doctrines, first, the division of the forms of government, and second, man's natural sociability.[66] Concerning the first, the teaching of our book in I, 1 (§§ 10-12) is to be compared with a number of "parallel" texts in the *Prima Secundae* of the *Summa*. The latter clearly indicates a more complete grasp of the Aristotelian doctrine which served as a source for both works. Since an author's development normally proceeds from a less to a more perfect stage, and not vice versa, the *De Regno* was therefore written before the *Prima Secundae*. Concerning the second point, we have in the prologue to the commentary on the Ethics a most interesting statement about natural sociability. This, compared with the parallel teaching in our work (I, 1, §§ 4-7), shows itself, again

[64] See the prologue of this work, ed. STEINER 3 f.
[65] Ed. DE POORTER 6.
[66] To what follows see below the references in I, 1, note 3, p. 4 and note 16, p. 7.

by reason of its greater doctrinal perfection and more competent utilization of the Aristotelian source, to be posterior to the *De Regno*. Now, according to recent research,[67] the writing of the *Prima Secundae* would seem to extend over the years 1268 to 1270; and the commentary on the Ethics was probably the first in the long series of Aristotelian commentaries[68] whose composition, according to TOLOMEO OF LUCCA,[69] commenced in the years when Aquinas was in Rome or near Rome, *i.e.*, A.D. 1265 and after. This clearly puts the *terminus ante quem* of the *De Regno* at around 1265. In this way, ECHARD's conclusion appears to be verified although, of course, only a relative chronology is obtained.

Our text also provides evidence as to the *terminus post quem* in that, to no small extent, it uses the Aristotelian Politics. The date of WILLIAM OF MOERBEKE's Latin translation of its eight books is established by means of the quotations as they appear in St. Thomas' works.[70] According to this criterion, it is to be set at around 1260, since in none of Aquinas' writings up to 1259, when the Master left his chair at the University of Paris and moved to Italy, is there any trace of a knowledge of the Politics. The year 1260 is therefore the *terminus post quem* for the *De Regno*. After that year quotations from the Politics begin to appear in St. Thomas, in *Contra Gentiles III*[71] as well as the *Lectura Super Matthaeum*[72] and the *De Regno*. Viewed from the angle of their relation to the Politics, these three works belong together and form within the totality of Aquinas' works a unit, distinctly different from the later writings, especially the moral part of the *Summa*. The latter reveals a thoroughgoing knowledge of the Politics, while in the former works this knowledge appears to be

[67] GLORIEUX 88, 94.   [68] GRABMANN, *Guglielmo di Moerbeke* 64.
[69] Text apud MANDONNET, *Ecrits* 60.

[70] G. VON HERTLING, *Zur Geschichte der Politik im Mittelalter;* quoted by GRABMANN, *Guglielmo di Moerbeke* 112.

[71] *CG* III, 22 = *Pol.* I, 8: 1256b 22; *ibid.* 81 = *Pol.* I, 5: 1254b 16-1255a 2.

[72] VIII, 2 (p. 120a) = *Pol.* I, 5: 1254b 4; X, 1 (p. 140a) = *Pol.* I, 8-9: 1256b 26, 40; XI, 2 (p. 157b) = *Pol.* I, 2: 1253a 27; XII, 2 (p. 170a) = *Pol.* I, 2: 1252b 12-30. It will be noted that the quotations from the Politics in the *De Regno* are much more numerous and taken from practically all its books. — The chronological problem of the *Lectura in Matth.* is far from being solved.

sporadic and based upon a cursory reading. It seems to be impossible to establish more definite chronological relations between these three works and thereby narrow down the date of composition of the *De Regno*. This, therefore, cannot be given more accurately than by the extreme termini 1260 and 1265.

St. Thomas and the Kingdom of Cyprus

The relations between St. Thomas and the Lusignan King were not of a personal character. It cannot be assumed, therefore, that the *De Regno* was written at an invitation from the Cypriote court, as later Boccaccio's *De Genealogiis Deorum* was composed at the invitation of Hugh IV of Cyprus[73] (1324-1358). It is more likely that the suggestion or request to address such a book to Hugh II came to Aquinas from one or the other of his Dominican brethren, either members of the Dominican Province of the Holy Land (*Provincia Terrae Sanctae*) or temporarily residing in its territory. One might think of names like Tommaso d'Agni di Lentino or Bl. Bartolomeo di Breganza.[74] The former was Aquinas' Prior in Naples when the young student received the Dominican habit (1244) and was twice in the Holy Land—from 1259 to 1263 as Bishop of Bethlehem and legate of the Holy See in the Orient, and from 1272 to 1277 as Patriarch of Jerusalem residing in St. Jean d'Acre. The latter was Bishop of Limassol (Nemesos) of Cyprus from 1250 to 1256, then returning to his native Italy. He was soon, however, employed in a Papal Mission to England, after which he went to Paris as St. Louis' guest during A.D. 1259-1260.

The *Provincia Terrae Sanctae* had its main quarters in Nicosia of Cyprus, the residence of the Lusignans.[75] The fact that Hugh II was the first and the only Lusignan king of the thirteenth century to be buried in St. Dominic's of Nicosia[76] is indicative of a special friendship between his house and the Dominicans around 1260. The Preachers are said to have settled in Nicosia around 1226, when Countess Alice d'Ibelin

[73] Hill 305, n. 2. [74] See *Script. O. P.* I, 358 ff, 254 ff.
[75] *Script. O. P.* XII.
[76] Stephen of Lusignan, *Chorograffia* f. 54, *Histoire* f. 17; quoted by Hill 157, n. 1.

gave them the site on which the church and convent were erected.[77] These buildings were rated among the finest examples of monastic architecture in the Latin Orient, comparable to the still existing monastery of the Augustinian canons, Bellapaïs of Cyprus. Did HUGH II, or someone of his family (perhaps the Queen-mother PLAISANCE OF ANTIOCH who was his guardian and Regent of the island until her death in 1261) give aid in the completion of these constructions? Was St. Thomas' *De Regno,* which the author characterizes as an "offering" to the king (*Cogitanti mihi quid offerrem* . . . § 1), an homage for services rendered and an expression of the Dominicans' gratitude for royal beneficence? We can neither affirm nor deny these assumptions.

The *Book On Kingship* might also, and perhaps at the same time, have been intended as a discreet incentive to services expected. The *Provincia Terrae Sanctae* was in the thirteenth century the most outstanding missionary unit of the Order, to every friar preacher an object of loving care, but also of grave concern. After the fall of Jerusalem A.D. 1244 and ST. LOUIS OF FRANCE's unsuccessful crusade, an increased activity of the Dominicans is noticeable to rally princes and peoples to the precarious cause of the Holy Land. TOMMASO D'AGNI addressed a circular letter to the sovereigns of Europe in 1260 and exposed in the same year the plight of Frankish Syria to CHARLES D'ANJOU.[78] There was no doubt that in a coming crusade the rôle of the King of Cyprus would have to be of primary importance, since the island was the natural base and starting-point for every military expedition beyond the sea. It is possible, then, that with the *De Regno* St. Thomas made his contribution to the great and urgent cause of Christendom, a contribution, as he says in § 1, "befitting my profession and office" (as a Dominican friar and a Master of theology). The original work might well have contained specific details about the idea and the urgency of the crusade (cf. §§ 119, 120).

Uncertain (but not unfounded) as these conjectures are, it will at any rate be useful to the modern reader to recapture, as precisely as possible, the connotations and implications

---

[77] STEPHEN OF LUSIGNAN, *Chorograffia* f. 32b; quoted by HILL 27.
[78] *Script. O. P.* I, 360. The first letter is inserted in the Chronicle of MENKO, pp. 547-549; the second published by H.-F. DELABORDE 211-215.

which the words "King of Cyprus," so prominently figuring
in the title of our book, had for St. Thomas as well as for any
mediaeval reader who took care to look at them. There is a great
deal of abstract teaching in the *De Regno*, but there are also
passages in which the author obviously intends to speak a
fairly concrete language and makes use of what he knows
about the political, economic, and geographical conditions in
the kingdom of Cyprus. The Franks were the lords and the
main element of the ruling class of the country and their
loyalty to their native land manifested itself at St. Louis of
France's arrival in Cyprus; the appeal to the old traditions of
Gaul in § 113 indicates that St. Thomas was well aware of
these facts. Further, the remark about slaves not forming
part of the civil community (§ 106), although directly due to
Aristotle,[79] points also to Cyprus and Frankish Syria and was
more readily understood in these lands of conquest, where
the cleavage between the conquering aliens and the hostile
natives had to be sharply emphasized. Wilbrand von Olden-
burg, author of a journal of pilgrimage A.D. 1211, presents the
following picture of the relations between the races in Cyprus
after the Frankish conquest:[80]

> The Greeks, over whom throughout this land the Latins
> have dominion, obey the Franks and pay tribute like
> slaves (*servi*). Whence you can see that the Franks
> are the lords of this land, whom the Greeks and
> Armenians obey as villeins (*coloni*). They are rude in
> all their ways, and go about poorly clothed, yet are
> given to self-indulgence (the blame for which may lie
> on the wine of Cyprus, or rather on those who drink it).

The picture of a degraded people, deprived of their civil
rights! A theory of human, if not civil, rights naturally remaining in conquered peoples (the theory which on the basis
of Thomistic principles was elaborated in the sixteenth century
by Francisco de Vitoria) did not come to St. Thomas' mind
on this occasion, as far as the remaining fragments of the *De
Regno* allow us to judge.

[79] See below II, 3, note 6, p. 60.
[80] Wilbrandi de Oldenborg, *Peregrinatio*: Cobham 13.

The much neglected, sometimes even ridiculed,[81] chapters 4-8 of the Second Book (= II, 1-4) also bear witness to Aquinas' care to take account of the conditions in Cyprus. The founding of a city and kingdom was indeed an opportunity characteristic of the crusading age. Was not the very kingdom of Cyprus, not long before St. Thomas' days, founded by a Lusignan who, beginning life as no more than a penniless, well-born adventurer, succeeded in establishing a reign which took root and flourished for three hundred years? Behind the lines of II, 6 (=II, 2) stands the city of Nicosia. It lies, according to the mediaeval travel account of LUDOLF VON SUDHEIM,[82]

under the mountains in a fine open plain with an excellent climate, where by reason of its well-tempered air and healthfulness the king and all the bishops and prelates of the realm, the princes and nobles and barons and knights, chiefly live.

But in other spots there were different climatic conditions as JACOBUS DE VERONA[83] relates:

... in that island the heat is such that in summer a man can scarcely live, and no one leaves his house except at night, and in the morning until the third hour, and from the hours of vespers onwards. I was nearly dead of that heat.

And of Famagusta, NICOLAUS DE MARTHONO[84] says:

One part of this city is close to the sea and another larger part is away from the sea; it is encompassed with very fine ditches built throughout. . . . Between the city of

---

[81]On St. Thomas' words in § 134 (*For the site of his kingdom the king ought to choose such a place as shall preserve the health of the inhabitants*) WILLIAM BARCLAY writes the following commentary: "Had this clever advice been given at the time of Noah's sons, or of Uranus, Saturnus and Janus, when the choice of dwelling places was wide open, the adviser should perhaps deserve being remembered as the Eighth Sage. But to say this in the thirteenth century, and to say it with an air of being serious, is either utter fatuity or stark madness. As though kingdoms were founded by a king going about the world and looking for a place that suits his caprice!" *De Regno et Regali Potestate* VI (A.D. 1600), quoted by FLORI 10. WILLIAM BARCLAY is one of the many who do not know how to read a mediaeval book.

[82] *De Terra Sancta et Itinere Jherosol.* (A.D. 1341): COBHAM 20.

[83] *Liber Peregrinationis* (A.D. 1335): COBHAM 17.

[84] *Liber Peregrinationis ad Loca Sancta* (A.D. 1394): COBHAM 24.

Famagusta and the ancient city of Constantia is a large
marsh which seems like an arm of the sea. And it is
held that on account of that marsh . . . a bad air affects
the men who dwell in that city.

It is perhaps on account of similar reports that St. Thomas
thought it advisable to remind the king of the ancient teaching
on the relation between civil life and climate and on the
importance of medicine for politics—a teaching of which St.
ALBERT says that from olden times it aroused the keenest
interest of the most potent kings and the most acute philosophers.[85]

The merchants receive a very stern treatment in II, 7
(=II, 3). Although the doctrine is of ecclesiastical, and even
classical, origin,[86] the reader should also recall, as Aquinas
certainly did, the ignominious events in St. Jean d'Acre during
1256-1258 when the greediness of the Genoese and the Vene-
tians and their commercial rivalries ruthlessly shattered what
little peace and unity St. LOUIS had been able to obtain in the
Frankish possessions of Syria. How appropriate is Aquinas'
warning to keep merchants in their place, written at a time
when the crusading spirit was dying out and trade was emerg-
ing as the attraction which led men towards the east. It is also
an almost prophetic warning. The later mediaeval history of
Cyprus shows the disastrous effects of the internecine struggle,
on the very soil of the island, between Venice and Genoa. The
following description by LUDOLF VON SUDHEIM[87] of Famagusta,
the richest mart in Christendom, and of its merchants, may
illustrate St. Thomas' views (although LUDOLF, an upright
Westphalian priest, did not visit Cyprus until between 1336
and 1341):

Famagusta is the richest of all cities, and her citizens
are the richest of men. A citizen once betrothed his
daughter, and the jewels of her headdress were valued
by the French knights who came with us as more
precious than all the ornaments of the Queen of France.
A certain merchant of this city sold to the Sultan a

[85] *De Natura Locorum* I, 7: IX, 342. The question of the habitability
of the different parts of the earth, especially of the Southern Hemis-
phere, is a "subject which never failed to appeal to the mediaeval
scholar or to reveal his intellectual calibre" (KIMBLE 84).
[86] See below II, 7, note 8, p. 76. [87] *Op. cit.*: COBHAM 19 f.

royal orb of gold, and thereon four precious stones, a
ruby, an emerald, a sapphire an-l a pearl, for sixty
thousand florins; and anon he sought to buy back that
orb for a hundred thousand florins, but it was denied
him. . . . In this city in one shop is more aloe wood than
five carts could carry away. I am silent concerning
spices, for they are as common there as bread is here,
and are sold as commonly. I dare not speak of their
precious stones and golden tissues and other riches, for
it were a thing unheard of and incredible. In this city
dwell very many wealthy courtesans, of whom some
possess more than one hundred thousand florins. I dare
not enlarge upon their riches.

The most precious example of St. Thomas' speaking to the
point is offered in II, 8 (=II, 4). There it is, the *Enchanted
Island*[58] where mediaeval exegesis located the vineyards of
Engaddi of the *Song of Songs* (i, 14: "my beloved is unto me as
a cluster of Cyprus in the vineyards of Engaddi").

I have heard from many of experience (says again
LUDOLF) that God has made for the use of men no fairer
or nobler ornament under the sun.

But beautiful Cyprus is also the land connected, in the
mediaeval mind, with the memory of the Aphrodite of classic
antiquity. To quote LUDOLF:[59]

Near Paphos once stood the castle of Venus, where
they were wont to adore an idol of Venus, and came to
visit its threshold from distant countries, and all noble
lords and ladies and damsels were gathered there. It
was there that counsel was first taken for the destruction
of Troy, for Helen was taken captive as she journeyed
thither. . . . In Cyprus above all lands men are by
nature more luxurious. For the soil of Cyprus of its
own self will provoke a man to lust.

If taken out of its hidden context, the transition in § 144 from
the description of a charming landscape to the warning against

---

[58] This is the title of W. H. MALLOCK's travel book, London, 1889.
Speaking, in § 137, of the "hazards of the sea ways," St. Thomas makes
it quite clear that he is addressing himself to an islander. The correct
reading *discrimina maris* was unfortunately lost through the incom-
petence of the scribes of the MSS.

[59] *Op. cit.*: COBHAM 13 f.

"indulgence in pleasures" might seem to be a bit of unwarrant-
ed moralizing and monkish bigotry, both very alien to the
balanced judgment of Aquinas. In fact, to avoid this impres-
sion, a number of variants were at this point inflicted upon
the original text by some later editors[90] who, in so doing, showed
their incapacity to read St. Thomas in any other than an
intransigently dogmatic fashion. But the passage becomes per-
fectly understandable when we know that, in the Middle Ages
as well as also much later, the Cypriotes' reputation in the
Occident was, as a mediaeval commentator of DANTE puts it,[91]
that they "overtopped all peoples of the kingdoms of Christendom in superfluity of luxury, gluttony, effeminacy and every
kind of pleasure."

The fragment on the theory of monarchy has also been
explained—but less successfully, it would seem—by usages and
events in the kingdom of Cyprus. MAURICE GRANDCLAUDE, in
an interesting note,[92] suggests that the De Regno "proclaims
the superiority of absolute monarchy and strongly takes
position against interference by the barons in the government." This would set our book against the Summa where a
"mixed government" is advocated.[93] The solution of the
Summa would be a universally valid statement while the
theory of the De Regno would appear to be construed ad hoc,
i.e., to help the king to overcome an acute crisis in which he
was in danger of being overthrown by his vassals. GEORGE
HILL even goes so far as to surmise that "the throne of Cyprus
was an experimental station in which principles commending themselves to the most active thinkers of their times could
be tested, with a chance of favourable results."[94] Yet, clearly,

[90] See the variants in Appendix I, § 143 ff, p. 90 ff.
[91] BENVENUTO DA IMOLA: COBHAM 15. — Chapter II, 8, thus, clearly
appears to have been written by the same author who addressed himself to the King of Cyprus. The so-called "continuation" of our book,
on the contrary, completely abandoned this original scope. In view,
therefore, of certain discussions about the authenticity of the chapters
II, 7 and 8 (ENDRES 262; see below II, 6, note 3, p. 73), it is interesting
to note that the beginning and the end of the treatise are clearly held
together by the same purpose.
[92] See Bull. Thom. 1930, p. 153 f.
[93] I-II, 105, 1. This discrepancy between the De Regno and the Summa
was much stressed by ENDRES 263-265. Cf. McILWAIN 331, n. 1.
[94] History of Cyprus 158.

there is no theory of absolute monarchy in the *De Regno*.[95] This book is not a stepping-stone to BODIN and MACHIAVELLI. In regard to its doctrine on monarchy, there is no opposition to the *Summa*.[96] The important § 42, although only a preliminary statement, shows with sufficient clarity that St. Thomas' ideal was a limited monarchy. The Cypriote monarchy was juridically ruled by the *Assises de Jérusalem* according to which sovereignty belonged in the last instance to a body of feudal barons, the *Haute Cour* or *Cour des Liges*, assembled in Nicosia, with the king presiding.[97] The decisions of this court were invested with an authority which was superior to that of the king alone. Only through this body, says L. DE MAS LATRIE, "a royal proposition received legal force; in this court all questions of succession to the throne, of minority and regency were settled; in the presence of the liege lords the identity of a new sovereign was to be recognized and his age and condition of birth probated, before, by the *Haute Cour* itself, he could receive the investiture with royal power."[98] One may hesitate to declare that the tenor of § 42 proves the author's knowledge of the text of the Assizes of Jerusalem. But there is hardly any doubt that the passage rests on precise information about the legal situation in the kingdom of Cyprus, and urges the principles of limited monarchy as laid down in that famous document. Far, therefore, from siding with certain "modern" and "progressive" attempts to strengthen monarchic power, which might (or might not) have materialized in Cyprus at the time of the composition of the *De Regno*, St. Thomas vigorously insists upon the traditional institution of a controlled and subordinated monarchy. In this he is in agreement with the most eminent Cypriote Jurist, JOHN D'IBELIN, Count of Jaffa. The *Livre de Jean d'Ibelin*, composed contemporaneously with the *De Regno*, contained a version of the Assizes of Jerusalem and "became by degrees the authoritative work of reference for the jurisprudence of the kingdom of Jerusalem and Cyprus."[99] Its general political philosophy is the same as that of Aquinas. It is clear also that this line of political thought

[95] See § 42, p. 24.   [96] Cf. CARLYLE V, 94; *and* I, 6, note 3, p. 24.
[97] On what follows cf. GROUSSET 503 ff.
[98] MAS LATRIE I, 129.   [99] HILL 165, 371.

was the only one that could be adopted by a Christian political thinker, for the limitation of political power is the very first and universally recognized preoccupation of **Christian Politics;** it is the essence and the driving power of the Christian revolution in the political field.   Had St. Thomas advocated the absolutism of royal power, he would have been guilty of pagan and reactionary tendencies.

*   *   *   *

From olden times, not a few readers have been disappointed with the book *On Kingship.* Its first editor trying to conceal the exact state of the fragments which he found among Aquinas' posthumous papers, the "continuator" piecing together two completely heterogeneous writings, the later editors boldly interfering with certain details of the text—all these show their dissatisfaction with the work as it stands, and in their many efforts to level off its edges and more or less discretely to palliate its difficulties, a very marked inability appears to grasp its peculiar character and value.

The book *On Kingship* ought to be read with a clear knowledge of its literary history and conditions. The circumstances of its composition as well as of its first edition should constantly be borne in mind. Further, let nobody expect it to be a full statement of Thomistic political or social doctrine. The book was written not for such a vast purpose but for the limited objective announced in the address and, consisting of no more than a few loose fragments, it does not even completely reveal the author's work with regard to this limited objective. Its chronology, moreover, conveys to the attentive reader the warning to use its statements with acumen and discernment: every doctrine expressed in it should be compared with a later text (if such is available) before a pronouncement is made in regard to what is to be considered as Aquinas' definitive and settled teaching. Above all, let the reader be careful to study St. Thomas' answers to St. Thomas' own problems; let nobody expect him to solve other and later questions of political science and practice. The *De Regno* is designed to enlighten a king in mediaeval Christendom; its teaching is deeply penetrated by the political atmosphere of thirteenth-century Europe. It should therefore, in the first place, be understood on its own premises and upon its immediate historical background. Only when, after careful examination, its relative validity is clearly perceived, will it be possible correctly to estimate the absolute value of its main principles. The profound spiritual significance of the fragment *De Regno*, its innermost soul and the final law of all its teaching, lies in the thesis that civil society is an institution founded upon nature and serving, in its own way and at a definite and inalienable place in human affairs, the ultimate end of man, the eternal salvation of his immortal soul. This thesis is an extension of St. Thomas' great theology of nature and grace, expressed in the historical situation of mediaeval Christendom and explicated by the notions and principles of Aristotelian philosophy. For having, especially in II, 3 (I, 14), coined the profoundest and clearest formula of the mediaeval City of God, the book *On Kingship* rightfully ranks as a classic in the world's political literature.

ON KINGSHIP

TO THE KING OF CYPRUS

To the King of Cyprus

[1] As I was turning over in my mind[1] what I might present to Your Majesty as a gift at once worthy of Your Royal Highness and befitting my profession and office, it seemed to me a highly appropriate offering that, for a king, I should write a book on kingship, in which, so far as my ability permits, I should carefully expound, according to the authority of Holy Writ and the teachings of the philosophers as well as the practice of worthy princes,[2] both the origin of kingly government and the things which pertain to the office of a king, relying for the beginning, progress and accomplishment of this work, on the help of Him, Who is King of Kings, Lord of Lords, through Whom kings rule, God the Mighty Lord, King great above all gods.[3]

[1] *Cogitanti mihi* . . . This beginning is also that of Cicero's *De Oratore*. It is sometimes used by mediaeval writers. See Thorndyke-Kibre 105.

[2] Cf. the prologue in Vincent of Beauvais' *De Eruditione Filiorum Nobilium*, p. 3.

[3] *Apoc.* xvii, 4; *Deut.* x, 17; *Proverb.* viii, 15; *Ps.* xciv, 3.

BOOK ONE

CHAPTER I

What Is Meant by the Word 'King'

[2] The first step in our undertaking must be to set forth what is to be understood by the term *king*.

[3] In all things which are ordered towards an end, wherein this or that course may be adopted, some directive principle is needed through which the due end may be reached by the most direct route. A ship, for example, which moves in different directions according to the impulse of the changing winds, would never reach its destination were it not brought to port by the skill of the pilot. Now, man has an end to which his whole life and all his actions are ordered; for man is an intelligent agent, and it is clearly the part of an intelligent agent to act in view of an end. Men also adopt different methods in proceeding towards their proposed end, as the diversity of men's pursuits and actions clearly indicates. Consequently man needs some directive principle to guide him towards his end.

[4] To be sure, the light of reason is placed by nature in every man, to guide him in his acts towards his end. Wherefore, if man were intended to live alone, as many animals do, he would require no other guide to his end. Each man would be a king unto himself, under

4 ON KINGSHIP

God, the highest King, inasmuch as he would direct
himself in his acts by the light of reason given him
from on high. Yet it is natural for man, more than
for any other animal,[1] to be a social and political
animal,[2] to live in a group.
[5] This is clearly a necessity of man's nature.[3] For
all other animals, nature has prepared food, hair as a
covering, teeth, horns, claws as means of defence or
at least speed in flight, while man alone was made
without any natural provisions for these things. Instead of all these, man was endowed with reason, by
the use of which he could procure all these things for
himself by the work of his hands.[4] Now, one man
alone is not able to procure them all for himself, for
one man could not sufficiently provide for life, un-
assisted. It is therefore natural that man should live
in the society of many.
[6] Moreover, all other animals are able to discern,
by inborn skill, what is useful and what is injurious,
even as the sheep naturally regards the wolf as his
enemy. Some animals also recognize by natural skill

[1] ARISTOTLE, Pol. I, 2: 1253a 8.
[2] ARISTOTLE, Hist. Anim. I, 1: 488a 7; Eth. Nic. I, 5; 1097b 11; ibid. IX,
9: 1169b 18; Pol. I, 2: 1253a 3. The Aristotelian formula is always that
man is a political animal. Unless special reasons suggested to Aquinas
the exact textual reproduction of this Aristotelian principle, he gen-
erally prefers to say that man is a social animal (SENECA, De Beneficiis
VII, 1, 7). The combination social and political animal is also found
in Summa I-II, 72, 4; In Periherm. I, 2.
[3] The source of the teaching in §§ 5-7 is not the Aristotelian Politics
but AVICENNA, De Anima V, 1; cf. C. Imp. 5 (*I, p. 94; henceforth the
asterisk and a Roman number refer to the texts translated in Append.
II). See also In Eth. prol. 4 (*II, p. 95) where St. Thomas, following
more closely the Aristotelian doctrine of Pol. I, 2: 1252b 30-1253a 18
(see *III, p. 96), no longer believes the Avicennian reasoning to be
capable of demonstrating the conclusion that man is a political animal.
Avicenna's argument is used by Aquinas in 4 Sent., 26, I, 1; Quodl.
VII, 17; CG III, 85 and ibid. 128, 129, 136, 147; Summa I-II, 95, 1.
[4] ARISTOTLE, De Partibus Animalium IV, 10: 687a 19. Cf. 3 Sent., I, 2,
sol. 1 ad 3; C. Imp. 5 (*I, p. 94); Quodl; VII, 17; Summa II-II, 187, 2 c.
and ad 1.

certain medicinal herbs and other things necessary
for their life. Man, on the contrary, has a natural
knowledge of the things which are essential for his
life only in a general fashion, inasmuch as he is able
to attain knowledge of the particular things necessary
for human life by reasoning from natural principles.
But it is not possible for one man to arrive at a
knowledge of all these things by his own individual
reason. It is therefore necessary for man to live in a
multitude so that each one may assist his fellows, and
different men may be occupied in seeking, by their
reason, to make different discoveries—one, for example, in medicine, one in this and another in that.

[7] This point is further and most plainly evidenced
by the fact that the use of speech is a prerogative
proper to man. By this means, one man is able fully
to express his conceptions to others. Other animals,
it is true, express their feelings to one another in a
general way, as a dog may express anger by barking
and other animals give vent to other feelings in various
fashions. But man communicates with his kind more
completely than any other animal known to be gregarious, such as the crane, the ant or the bee.⁵—With
this in mind, Solomon says: "It is better that there be
two than one; for they have the advantage of their
company."⁶

[8] If, then, it is natural for man to live in the society
of many, it is necessary that there exist among men
some means by which the group may be governed.
For where there are many men together and each one
is looking after his own interest, the multitude would
be broken up and scattered unless there were also an
agency to take care of what appertains to the common-

ON KINGSHIP

weal. In like manner, the body of a man or any other animal would disintegrate unless there were a general ruling force within the body which watches over the common good of all members.—With this in mind, Solomon says: "Where there is no governor, the people shall fall."[7]

[9] Indeed it is reasonable that this should happen, for what is proper and what is common are not identical.[8] Things differ by what is proper to each: they are united by what they have in common. But diversity of effects is due to diversity of causes. Consequently, there must exist something which impels towards the common good of the many, over and above that which impels towards the particular good of each individual. Wherefore also in all things that are ordained towards one end, one thing is found to rule the rest.[9] Thus in the corporeal universe, by the first body, *i.e.* the celestial body, the other bodies are regulated according to the order of Divine Providence; and all bodies are ruled by a rational creature.[10] So, too, in the individual man, the soul rules the body; and among the parts of the soul, the irascible and the concupiscible parts are ruled by reason.[11] Likewise, among the members of a body, one, such as the heart or the head,[12] is the principal and moves all the others. Therefore in every multitude there must be some governing power.

[10] Now it happens in certain things which are ordained towards an end that one may proceed in a

[7] *Prov.* xi, 14.   [8] Cf. *Summa* I, 96, 4.
[9] ARISTOTLE, *Pol.* I, 5: 1254a 28. — *In Metaph. prol.; In I Tim.* II, 3 (p. 197a); *Summa* I, 96, 4.
[10] Cf. *CG* III, 23; *ibid.*, 78.
[11] *Summa* I, 81, 3 ad 2; I-II, 9, 2 ad 3; *ibid.*, 17, 2 in 2, 7 *in corp.*, and often elsewhere.
[12] ARISTOTLE, *Metaph. Delta* 1: 1013a 5. — *In Met.* V, 1: 755.

right way and also in a wrong way. So, too, in the government of a multitude there is a distinction between right and wrong.[13] A thing is rightly directed when it is led towards a befitting end; wrongly when it is led towards an unbefitting end. Now the end which befits a multitude of free men is different from that which befits a multitude of slaves, for the free man is one who exists for his own sake, while the slave, as such, exists for the sake of another.[14] If, therefore, a multitude of free men is ordered by the ruler towards the common good of the multitude, that rulership will be right and just, as is suitable to free men. If, on the other hand, a rulership aims, not at the common good of the multitude, but at the private good of the ruler, it will be an unjust and perverted rulership. The Lord, therefore, threatens such rulers, saying by the mouth of Ezechiel:[15] "Woe to the shepherds that feed themselves (seeking, that is, their own interest): should not the flocks be fed by the shepherd?" Shepherds indeed should seek the good of their flocks, and every ruler, the good of the multitude subject to him.

[11] If an unjust government is carried on by one man alone,[16] who seeks his own benefit from his rule

---

[13] Aristotle, Pol. III, 6: 1279a 17; Eth. Nic. VIII, 10: 1160a 31. — In Eth. VIII, 10 (*IV, p. 98); In Pol. III 5 (*V, p. 101).

[14] Aristotle, Metaph. Alpha 2: 982b 25.

[15] xxxiv, 2.

[16]The classification of constitutions in §§ 11-12 is owed to Aristotle, Pol. III, 7: 1279a 27 ff. The basis of number, however, on which this classification rests, is found inadequate by Aristotle himself ibid. 1279b 38. In later texts, St. Thomas gradually abandoned it; see In Eth. VIII, 10 (*IV, p. 98); Summa I-II, 95, 4; ibid., 105, 1; II-II, 50, 1, arg. 1; ibid., 61 2; In Pol. III, 6 (*V, p. 101). St. Thomas ends up, just as Aristotle did, with a list of constitutions in which each finds its essential characteristic in a certain qualification on account of which political power is awarded: in monarchy and aristocracy, power is given on account of virtue, in oligarchy on account of riches, in democracy on account of liberty. See Newman I, 220.

and not the good of the multitude subject to him, such a ruler is called a *tyrant* — a word derived from *strength*[17]—because he oppresses by might instead of ruling by justice. Thus among the ancients all powerful men were called tyrants. If an unjust government is carried on, not by one but by several, and if they be few, it is called an *oligarchy*, that is, the rule of a few. This occurs when a few, who differ from the tyrant only by the fact that they are more than one, oppress the people by means of their wealth. If, finally, the bad government is carried on by the multitude, it is called a *democracy, i.e.* control by the populace, which comes about when the plebeian people by force of numbers oppress the rich. In this way the whole people will be as one tyrant.

[12] In like manner we must divide just governments. If the government is administered by many, it is given the name common to all forms of government, *viz. polity*, as for instance when a group of warriors exercise dominion over a city or province.[18] If it is administered by a few men of virtue, this kind of government is called an *aristocracy, i.e.* noble governance, or governance by noble men, who for this reason are called the *Optimates*.[19] And if a just government is in the hands of one man alone, he is properly called a *king*. Wherefore the Lord says by the mouth

[17] St. Isidore of Seville, *Etymologiae* IX, 19: PL 82, 344. St. Augustine, *De Civ. Dei* V, 19.

[18] The meaning of this proposition, which is doubtlessly intended to be a reproduction of *Pol.* III, 7: 1279b 1, is not clear. Aristotle says *loco cit.*: "There is a good reason for the usage [which gives to this form of government the generic name *Polity*.] It is possible for one man, or a few, to be of outstanding excellence, but when it comes to a large number, we can hardly expect a fine edge of all the varieties of excellence. What we can expect is the military kind of excellence, which is the kind that shows itself in a mass" (Transl. Barker.) See *In Pol.* III, 6 (*V, p. 101).

[19] Cf. Cicero, *Pro P. Sestio* 45, 36; Id., *De Officiis* II, 23, 80.

of Ezechiel:[20] "My servant, David, shall be king over them and all of them shall have one shepherd."

[13] From this it is clearly shown that the idea of king implies that he be one man who is chief and that he be a shepherd seeking the common good of the multitude and not his own.

[14] Now since man must live in a group, because he is not sufficient unto himself to procure the necessities of life were he to remain solitary, it follows that a society will be the more perfect the more it is sufficient unto itself to procure the necessities of life.[21] There is, to some extent, sufficiency for life in one *family of one household,* namely, insofar as pertains to the natural acts of nourishment and the begetting of offspring and other things of this kind. Self-sufficiency exists, furthermore, in one *street*[22] with regard to those things which belong to the trade of one guild. In a *city,* which is the perfect community, it exists with regard to all the necessities of life. Still more

---

[20] xxvii, 24.

[21] ARISTOTLE *Pol.* I, 2: 1252b 9-30; *In Pol.* I, 1 (*III, p. 96). The Aristotelian doctrine is here adapted to mediaeval realities in almost the same fashion as in some other earlier writings of Aquinas: *In Matth.* XII, 2 (p. 170a); *In Ioan.* XIV, 1, 3 (p. 377a); *In I Cor.* XI, 4 (p. 333a); *In Hebr.* XI, 3 (p. 414a). In the later writings, Aquinas (a) more clearly emphasizes the fact that the Aristotelian city seeks the satisfaction of not only the material but also the moral needs of man: *In Eth. prol.* (*II, p. 95); *Summa* I-II, 90, 2; cf. *infra* § 106, p. 59. Moreover (b) he treats cities and kingdoms not as specifically different communities each having its own essential characteristics, but as formally equal and only materially, i.e., historically different realizations of the same idea of "perfect community". Proof of this is the use of the combination *city or kingdom* in *Summa* II-II, 47, 11; *ibid.* 50, 1; *ibid.* 3 — On mediaeval opinions and texts in this matter see GIERKE-MAITLAND 21, 129.

[22] In Latin *vicus.* This is neither here nor *In Pol.* I, 1 (*III, p. 96) the Aristotelian clan-village but the street of the mediaeval town, called *vicus (v.g. Vicus Straminis).* In each street, St. Thomas says *In Pol.* (*III, p. 96), "one craft is exercised, in one the weaver's, in another the smith's." Modern towns still preserve the memory of this mediaeval arrangement in street names such as Shoemaker Row, Cordwainer Street, Comerslane, Butter Row etc.

self-sufficiency is found in a *province*[23] because of the
need of fighting together and of mutual help against
enemies. Hence the man ruling a perfect community,
i.e. a city or a province, is antonomastically[24] called *the*
king. The ruler of a household is called father, not
king, although he bears a certain resemblance to the
king,[25] for which reason kings are sometimes called
the fathers of their peoples.

[15] It is plain, therefore, from what has been said,
that a king is one who rules the people of one city or
province, and rules them for the common good. Wherefore Solomon says:[26] "The king ruleth over all the
land subject to him."

[23] The word is of Roman imperial origin; cf. St. Isidore, *Etymologiae*
XIV, 3, 19. It is also used in mediaeval Canon Law; see Gratian's
Decretum c. 2 C. VI, p. 3: an ecclesiastical province is a territory where
there are ten or eleven cities, one king . . . , one metropolitan . . .
In St. Albert's cosmography (*De Nat. Locorum* III, 1 ff: IX, 566 ff)
Italy "is a province" but it also "contains several provinces", *viz.*, Cala-
bria, Apulia, Romana, Emilia, Tuscia, Lombardia. Likewise, Spain is a
province and "has several provinces and kingdoms." See St. Thomas'
use of the word in 2 *Sent.*, 10, I, 3 *ad* 3; 4 *Sent.*, 24, III, 2 *sol.* 3; *Summa*
II-II, 40, 1. — Nothing is very definite about this notion except that, at
any rate, a province is part of a greater and more comprehensive whole.
The word is therefore characteristic of a properly mediaeval type of
political thinking which still retains the memory of the Roman
Empire. It was soon to be cast out of the political vocabulary; see
John of Paris, *De Pot. Regia et Papali* I, 1; ed. Leclercq 176/7.

[24] Antonomasia is the figure of speech by which a generic predicate
is used to designate an individual because it belongs to this individual
in an eminent degree; for instance: Rome is *the* city (*Summa* II-II,
125, 2); divine truth is *the* truth (*CG* I, 1.)

[25] Aristotle, *Eth. Nic.* VIII, 12: 1160b 24; *In Eth.* VIII, 10: 1682.

[26] *Eccles.* v, 8.

CHAPTER II

WHETHER IT IS MORE EXPEDIENT FOR A CITY OR PROVINCE TO BE RULED BY ONE MAN OR BY MANY

[16] Having set forth these preliminary points we must now inquire what is better for a province or a city: whether to be ruled by one man or by many.

[17] This question may be considered first from the viewpoint of the purpose of government. The aim of any ruler should be directed towards securing the welfare of that which he undertakes to rule. The duty of the pilot, for instance, is to preserve his ship amidst the perils of the sea and to bring it unharmed to the port of safety. Now the welfare and safety of a multitude formed into a society lies in the preservation of its unity, which is called peace. If this is removed, the benefit of social life is lost and, moreover, the multitude in its disagreement becomes a burden to itself. The chief concern of the ruler of a multitude, therefore, is to procure the unity of peace.[1] It is not even legitimate for him to deliberate whether he shall establish peace in the multitude subject to him, just as a physician does not deliberate whether he shall heal the sick man encharged to him,[2] for no one should deliberate about an end which he is obliged to seek, but only about the means to attain that end. Where-

---

[1] *CG* I, 42, IV, 76; *Summa* I, 103, 3. This idea is characteristic of Hellenistic political philosophy, according to which the main function of the King-Saviour is considered to be the establishment of order and peace. Cf. P. WENDLAND 143 f. Also ST. AUGUSTINE, *De Civitate Dei* XIX, 12 ff; DIONYSIUS (Ps.-AREOPAGITE), *De Divinis Nominibus* XI: PG 3, 935 ff (St. Thomas *in h. l.*, pp. 601 ff, esp. 613 ff.)

[2] ARISTOTLE *Eth. Nic.* III, 5: 1112b 14 (Latin text). *In Eth.* III, 8: 474; *CG* III, 146; *In Matth.* XII, 2: p. 170a. In thus tracing back to ARISTOTLE the idea that peace is the chief social good, St. Thomas was misled by the fact that the Latin text of the Ethics translated the Greek *EUNOMIA* (good laws well obeyed) by *peace*.

fore the Apostle, having commended the unity of the faithful people, says:[3] "Be ye careful to keep the unity of the spirit in the bond of peace." Thus, the more efficacious a government is in keeping the unity of peace, the more useful it will be. For we call that more useful which leads more directly to the end. Now it is manifest that what is itself one can more efficaciously bring about unity than several[4]—just as the most efficacious cause of heat is that which is by its nature hot. Therefore the rule of one man is more useful than the rule of many.

[18] Furthermore, it is evident that several persons could by no means preserve the stability of the community if they totally disagreed. For union is necessary among them if they are to rule at all: several men, for instance, could not pull a ship in one direction unless joined together in some fashion. Now several are said to be united according as they come closer to being one. So one man rules better than several who come near being one.[5]

[19] Again, whatever is in accord with nature is best, for in all things nature does what is best. Now, every natural governance is governance by one.[6] In the multitude of bodily members there is one which is the principal mover, namely, the heart; and among the powers of the soul one power presides as chief, namely, the reason. Among bees there is one king bee[7] and in the whole universe there is One God, Maker and Ruler of all things. And there is a reason for this. Every multitude is derived from unity.

[3] *Ephes.* iv, 3.   [4] *CG* IV, 76; *Summa* I, 103, 3.
[5] *In Eth.* VIII, 10 (*IV, p. 98).
[6] See above § 9, p. 6; CG I, 42.
[7] In popular ancient and mediaeval opinion the chief bee was considered to be a male. ARISTOTLE, *Hist. Anim.* V, 21: 553a 25.

Wherefore, if artificial things are an imitation of natural things[8] and a work of art is better according as it attains a closer likeness to what is in nature, it follows that it is best for a human multitude to be ruled by one person.

[20] This is also evident from experience. For provinces or cities which are not ruled by one person are torn with dissensions and tossed about without peace, so that the complaint seems to be fulfilled which the Lord uttered through the Prophet:[9] "Many pastors have destroyed my vineyard." On the other hand, provinces and cities which are ruled under one king enjoy peace, flourish in justice, and delight in prosperity. Hence, the Lord by His prophets promises to His people as a great reward that He will give them one head and that "one Prince will be in the midst of them."[10]

CHAPTER III

THAT THE DOMINION OF A TYRANT IS THE WORST

[21] Just as the government of a king is the best, so the government of a tyrant is the worst.[1]

[22] For democracy stands in contrary opposition to polity, since both are governments carried on by many persons, as is clear from what has already been said;[2] while oligarchy is the opposite of aristocracy, since both are governments carried on by a few persons; and kingship is the opposite of tyranny since both are carried on by one person. Now, as has been

---

[8] ARISTOTLE, *Phys.* II, 2: 194a 21.
[9] *Jerem.* xii, 10.   [10] *Ezech.* xxxiv, 24; *Jerem.* xxx, 21.
[1] ARISTOTLE, *Eth. Nic.* VIII, 12: 1160a 35. b 8; *In Eth.* VIII, 10 (*IV, p. 98).   [2] Ch. I, 11-12, p. 7 ff.

shown above,³ monarchy is the best government. If, therefore, "it is the contrary of the best that is worst"⁴ it follows that tyranny is the worst kind of government. [23] Further, a united force is more efficacious in producing its effect than a force which is scattered or divided. Many persons together can pull a load which could not be pulled by each one taking his part separately and acting individually. Therefore, just as it is more useful for a force operating for a good to be more united, in order that it may work good more effectively, so a force operating for evil is more harmful when it is one than when it is divided. Now, the power of one who rules unjustly works to the detriment of the multitude, in that he diverts the common good of the multitude to his own benefit. Therefore, for the same reason that, in a just government, the government is better in proportion as the ruling power is one—thus monarchy is better than aristocracy, and aristocracy better than polity—so the contrary will be true of an unjust government, namely, that the ruling power will be more harmful in proportion as it is more unitary. Consequently, tyranny is more harmful than oligarchy; and oligarchy more harmful than democracy.

[24] Moreover, a government becomes unjust by the fact that the ruler, paying no heed to the common good, seeks his own private good. Wherefore the further he departs from the common good the more unjust will his government be. But there is a greater departure from the common good in an oligarchy, in which the advantage of a few is sought, than in a democracy, in which the advantage of many is sought; and there is a still greater departure from the common

³Ch. II, p. 11 ff.   ⁴ ARISTOTLE, Eth. Nic. VIII, 12: 1160b 9.

good in a tyranny, where the advantage of only one man is sought. For a large number is closer to the totality than a small number, and a small number than only one. Thus, the government of a tyrant is the most unjust.

[25] The same conclusion is made clear to those who consider the order of Divine Providence, which disposes everything in the best way. In all things, good ensues from one perfect cause, i.e. from the totality of the conditions favourable to the production of the effect, while evil results from any one partial defect.[5] There is beauty in a body when all its members are fittingly disposed; ugliness, on the other hand, arises when any one member is not fittingly disposed. Thus ugliness results in different ways from many causes; beauty in one way from one perfect cause. It is thus with all good and evil things, as if God so provided that good, arising from one cause, be stronger, and evil, arising from many causes, be weaker. It is expedient therefore that a just government be that of one man only in order that it may be stronger; however, if the government should turn away from justice, it is more expedient that it be a government by many, so that it may be weaker and the many may mutually hinder one another. Among unjust governments, therefore, democracy is the most tolerable, but the worst is tyranny.

[26] This same conclusion is also apparent if one considers the evils which come from tyrants. Since a tyrant, despising the common good, seeks his private interest, it follows that he will oppress his subjects in different ways according as he is dominated by differ-

---

[5]DIONYSIUS (Ps.-AREOPAGITE), *De Div. Nom.* IV, 30: PG 3, 729; St. *Thomas in h. l.* (IV, 22), p. 461.

ent passions to acquire certain goods. The one who is enthralled by the passion of cupidity seizes the goods of his subjects; whence Solomon says:[6] "A just king setteth up the land; a covetous man shall destroy it." If he is dominated by the passion of anger, he sheds blood for nothing; whence it is said by Ezechiel:[7] "Her princes in the midst of her are like wolves ravening the prey to shed blood." Therefore this kind of government is to be avoided as the Wise man admonishes:[8] "Keep thee far from the man who has the power to kill," because, forsooth, he kills not for justice' sake but by his power, for the lust of his will. Thus there can be no safety. Everything is uncertain when there is a departure from justice. Nobody will be able firmly to state: This thing is such and such, when it depends upon the will of another, not to say upon his caprice. Nor does the tyrant merely oppress his subjects in corporal things but he also hinders their spiritual good. Those who seek more to use, than to be of use to, their subjects prevent all progress, suspecting all excellence in their subjects to be prejudicial to their own evil domination. For tyrants hold the good in greater suspicion than the wicked, and to them the valour of others is always fraught with danger.[9]

[27] So the above-mentioned[10] tyrants strive to pre-

---

[6] *Prov.* xxix, 4.   [7] xxii, 27.   [8] *Eccli.* ix, 18.

[9] This sentence occurs word for word in SALLUST, *Bellum Catilinae* VII, 2 where, however, it is said of kings. It is the sentence immediately preceding the one quoted below in § 31, p. 19. This plagiarism is most unusual in St. Thomas' writings.

[10] In Latin: *praedicti tyranni.* § 27 is a reproduction of ARISTOTLE'S account of the traditional tyrant's policy of repression, "many of whose characteristics are supposed to have been instituted by PERIANDER OF CORINTH; but many may also be derived from the Persian government" (*Pol.* V, 11: 1313a 35-1314a 29). It is perhaps not unreasonable to think of the possibility that St. Thomas' original carried a mention of PERIANDER and the Persian tyrants. On this supposition it would be easier to explain the surprising reference to names or persons which have not been mentioned.

vent those of their subjects who have become virtuous
from acquiring valour and high spirit in order that
they may not want to cast off their iniquitous domination. They also see to it that there be no friendly relations among these so that they may not enjoy the
benefits resulting from being on good terms with one
another, for as long as one has no confidence in the
other, no plot will be set up against the tyrant's domination. Wherefore they sow discords among the
people, foster any that have arisen, and forbid anything which furthers society and co-operation among
men, such as marriage, company at table and anything
of like character, through which familiarity and confidence are engendered among men. They moreover
strive to prevent their subjects from becoming powerful and rich since, suspecting these to be as wicked
as themselves, they fear their power and wealth; for
the subjects might become harmful to them even as
they are accustomed to use power and wealth to harm
others.[11] Whence in the *Book of Job*[12] it is said of the
tyrant: "The sound of dread is always in his ears and
when there is peace (that is, when there is no one to
harm him), he always suspects treason."

[28] It thus results that when rulers, who ought to
induce their subjects to virtue,[13] are wickedly jealous
of the virtue of their subjects and hinder it as much
as they can, few virtuous men are found under the

[11]Although there is no doubt about the fact that *Pol. l. c.* (note 10)
is the source of this §, yet the text cannot be shown to depend literally
on this source. Cf. SUSEMIHL 573-579. A disturbing feature of this
paraphrase is that the author makes it a point of the tyrant's policy
to "forbid marriage". No trace of such a prohibition is to be found
in ARISTOTLE's account or its mediaeval version. St. Thomas is usually
very accurate even in the most trifling details of his quotations.
[12] xv, 21.
[13]ARISTOTLE, *Eth. Nic.* II, 1: 1103b 3. *In Eth.* II, 1: 251; *Summa* I-II,
95, 1.

18 ON KINGSHIP

rule of tyrants. For, according to ARISTOTLE's sentence, brave men are found where brave men are honoured.[14] And as TULLIUS[15] says: "Those who are despised by everybody are disheartened and flourish but little." It is also natural that men, brought up in fear, should become mean of spirit and discouraged in the face of any strenuous and manly task. This is shown by experience in provinces that have long been under tyrants. Hence the Apostle says to the Colossians:[16] "Fathers, provoke not your children to indignation, lest they be discouraged."

[29] So, considering these evil effects of tyranny, King Solomon says:[17] "When the wicked reign, men are ruined" because, forsooth, through the wickedness of tyrants, subjects fall away from the perfection of virtue. And again he says:[18] "When the wicked shall bear rule the people shall mourn, as though led into slavery." And again:[19] "When the wicked rise up men shall hide themselves", that they may escape the cruelty of the tyrant. It is no wonder, for a man governing without reason, according to the lust of his soul, in no way differs from the beast. Whence Solomon says:[20] "As a roaring lion and a hungry bear, so is a wicked prince over the poor people." Therefore men hide from tyrants as from cruel beasts and it seems that to be subject to a tyrant is the same thing as to lie prostrate beneath a raging beast.

[14] *Eth. Nic.* III, 11: 1116a 20. *In Eth.* III, 16: 562.
[15] *Tuscul. Disp.* I, 2, 4. [16] *Col.* iii, 21. [17] *Prov.* xxviii, 12.
[18] *Prov.* xxix, 2. [19] *Prov.* xxviii, 28. [20] *Prov.* xxviii, 15.

CHAPTER IV

Why the Royal Dignity Is Rendered Hateful to the Subjects

[30] Because both the best and the worst government are latent in monarhy, *i.e.* in the rule of one man, the royal dignity is rendered hateful to many people on account of the wickedness of tyrants. Some men, indeed, whilst they desire to be ruled by a king, fall under the cruelty of tyrants, and not a few rulers exercise tyranny under the cloak of royal dignity.

[31] A clear example of this is found in the Roman Republic. When the kings had been driven out by the Roman people, because they could not bear the royal, or rather tyrannical, arrogance, they instituted consuls and other magistrates by whom they began to be ruled and guided.[1] They changed the kingdom into an aristocracy, and, as Sallust[2] relates: "The Roman city, once liberty was won, waxed incredibly strong and great in a remarkably short time." For it frequently happens that men living under a king strive more sluggishly for the common good, inasmuch as they consider that what they devote to the common good, they do not confer upon themselves but upon another, under whose power they see the common goods to be. But when they see that the common good is not under the power of one man, they do not attend to it as if it belonged to another, but each one attends to it as if it were his own.[3]

[32] Experience thus teaches that one city administered by rulers, changing annually, is sometimes able

---

[1] St. Augustine, *De Civ. Dei* V, 12; Sallust, *Bellum Catilinae* VI, 7.
[2] St. Augustine, *l.c.* Sallust, *l.c.*   [3] Cf. *Summa* I-II, 105, 1.

to do more than some kings having, perchance, two or three cities; and small services exacted by kings weigh more heavily than great burdens imposed by the community of citizens. This held good in the history of the Roman Republic. The plebs were enrolled in the army and were paid wages for military service.⁴ Then when the common treasury was failing, private riches came forth for public uses, to such an extent that not even the senators retained any gold for themselves save one ring and the one *bulla* (the insignia of their dignity).

[33] On the other hand, when the Romans were worn out by continual dissensions taking on the proportion of civil wars, and when by these wars the freedom for which they had greatly striven was snatched from their hands, they began to find themselves under the power of emperors who, from the beginning, were unwilling to be called kings, for the royal name was hateful to the Romans. Some emperors, it is true, faithfully cared for the common good in a kingly manner, and by their zeal the commonwealth was increased and preserved. But most of them became tyrants towards their subjects while indolent and vacillating before their enemies, and brought the Roman commonwealth to naught.⁵

[34] A similar process took place, also, among the Hebrew people. At first, while they were ruled by judges, they were ravished by their enemies on every hand, for each one "did what was good in his sight."⁶ Yet when, at their own pressing, God gave them kings,⁷

---

⁴This and the subsequent propositions are taken from St. Augustine, *De Civ. Dei* III, 19 (Livy XXVI, 36). The golden *bulla* is an ornament of the noble or rich Roman youth, consisting of a lenticular plate which was worn hanging upon the breast: Pauly-Wissowa III, 1048.
⁵ Cf. St. Augustine, *De Civ. Dei* V, 12.
⁶ I. *Kings* iii, 18.   ⁷ I. *Kings* xii, 12, 13.

they departed from the worship of the one God and were finally led into bondage, on account of the wickedness of their kings.

[35] Danger thus lurks on either side. Either men are held by the fear of a tyrant and they miss the opportunity of having that very best government which is kingship; or, they want a king and the kingly power turns into tyrannical wickedness.

CHAPTER V

That It Is a Lesser Evil When a Monarchy Turns Into Tyranny Than When an Aristocracy Becomes Corrupt

[36] When a choice is to be made between two things, from both of which danger impends, surely that one should be chosen from which the lesser evil follows. Now, lesser evil follows from the corruption of a monarchy (which is tyranny) than from the corruption of an aristocracy.

[37] Group government [polyarchy] most frequently breeds dissension. This dissension runs counter to the good of peace which is the principal social good. A tyrant, on the other hand, does not destroy this good, rather he obstructs one or the other individual interest of his subjects—unless, of course, there be an excess of tyranny and the tyrant rages against the whole community. Monarchy is therefore to be preferred to polyarchy, although either form of government might become dangerous.

[38] Further, that from which great dangers may follow more frequently is, it would seem, the more to be avoided. Now, considerable dangers to the multitude follow more frequently from polyarchy than

from monarchy. There is a greater chance that, where there are many rulers, one of them will abandon the intention of the common good than that it will be abandoned when there is but one ruler. When any one among several rulers turns aside from the pursuit of the common good, danger of internal strife threatens the group because, when the chiefs quarrel, dissension will follow in the people. When, on the other hand, one man is in command, he more often keeps to governing for the sake of the common good. Should he not do so, it does not immediately follow that he also proceeds to the total oppression of his subjects. This, of course, would be the excess of tyranny and the worst wickedness in government, as has been shown above.[1] The dangers, then, arising from a polyarchy are more to be guarded against than those arising from a monarchy.

[39] Moreover, in point of fact, a polyarchy deviates into tyranny not less but perhaps more frequently than a monarchy. When, on account of there being many rulers, dissensions arise in such a government, it often happens that the power of one preponderates and he then usurps the government of the multitude for himself. This indeed may be clearly seen from history. There has hardly ever been a polyarchy that did not end in tyranny. The best illustration of this fact is the history of the Roman Republic. It was for a long time administered by the magistrates but then animosities, dissensions and civil wars arose and it fell into the power of the most cruel tyrants. In general,

---

[1]Ch. III, p. 13 ff. The statement in § 23: "tyranny is more harmful than oligarchy", is not contradictory to the thesis of the present chapter, as ENDRES, p. 266, affirms. The reasoning of ch. III proceeds on the supposition of an absolute and total tyranny, which is here expressly set aside.

if one carefully considers what has happened in the past[2] and what is happening in the present,[3] he will discover that more men have held tyrannical sway in lands previously ruled by many rulers than in those ruled by one.

[40] The strongest objection why monarchy, although it is "the best form of government", is not agreeable to the people is that, in fact, it may deviate into tyranny. Yet tyranny is wont to occur not less but more frequently on the basis of a polyarchy than on the basis of a monarchy. It follows that it is, in any case, more expedient to live under one king than under the rule of several men.[4]

CHAPTER VI

How Provision Might Be Made that the King May Not Fall Into Tyranny

[41] Therefore, since the rule of one man, which is the best, is to be preferred, and since it may happen that it be changed into a tyranny, which is the worst (all this is clear from what has been said), a scheme should be carefully worked out which would prevent the multitude ruled by a king from falling into the hands of a tyrant.

[2] Cf. Aristotle, Pol. V, 12: 1316a 34-39.
[3] St. Thomas may here be thinking of the Italian city republics where an originally oligarchic constitution was often superseded by the one-man rule and the despotism of a faction-chief, i.e., a Podestà or a Captain (head of either the popolo or the militia.) Ezzelino, the Podestà of Padua, who exiled the Dominican Bishop Bartolomeo di Breganza, was Aquinas' contemporary. See The Cambr. Med. Hist. VI, 178 ff, 875 ff.
[4] On St. Thomas' whole doctrine of the superiority of kingship see Gilson, Thomisme 455 ff.

[42] First, it is necessary that the man who is raised up to be king by those whom it concerns should be of such condition that it is improbable that he should become a tyrant.[1] Wherefore Daniel,[2] commending the providence of God with respect to the institution of the king says: "The Lord hath sought him a man according to his own heart, and the Lord hath appointed him to be prince over his people." Then, once the king is established, the government of the kingdom must be so arranged that opportunity to tyrannize is removed. At the same time his power should be so tempered that he cannot easily fall into tyranny.[3] How these things may be done we must consider in what follows.[4]

[43] Finally, provision must be made for facing the situation should the king stray into tyranny.[5]

[44] Indeed, if there be not an excess of tyranny it is more expedient to tolerate the milder tyranny for a while than, by acting against the tyrant, to become involved in many perils more grievous than the tyranny itself. For it may happen that those who act against the tyrant are unable to prevail and the tyrant then will rage the more. But should one be able to prevail against the tyrant, from this fact itself very grave dissensions among the people frequently ensue: the multitude may be broken up into factions either during

[1] See Introduction p. xxxvii.   [2] I *Kings* xiii, 14.
[3] Cf. *Summa* I-II, 105, 1. CARLYLE (V, 94) correctly observes that, if these remarks had been completed, it would have been under terms similar to those on which in the *Summa*, l.c., a mixed constitution is recommended. — For a different interpretation see McILWAIN 330 f.
[4] See Introduction p. xviii.
[5] A similar problem is discussed in 2 *Sent.*, 44, II, 2 (*VI, p. 103) and *Summa* II-II, 42, 2 ad 3; cf. also *Summa* II-II, 64, 3. For the history of this problem see CARLYLE I, 147 ff, 161 ff, III, 115 ff. The considerations of the present chapter should also be read against the background of the history of the Italian Communes in the XIIIth century; see *Cambridge Med. Hist.* VI, 179 ff.

their revolt against the tyrant, or in process of the organization of the government, after the tyrant has been overthrown. Moreover, it sometimes happens that while the multitude is driving out the tyrant by the help of some man, the latter, having received the power, thereupon seizes the tyranny. Then, fearing to suffer from another what he did to his predecessor, he oppresses his subjects with an even more grievous slavery. This is wont to happen in tyranny, namely, that the second becomes more grievous than the one preceding, inasmuch as, without abandoning the previous oppressions, he himself thinks up fresh ones from the malice of his heart. Whence in Syracuse, at a time when everyone desired the death of Dionysius, a certain old woman kept constantly praying that he might be unharmed and that he might survive her. When the tyrant learned this he asked why she did it. Then she said: "When I was a girl we had a harsh tyrant and I wished for his death; when he was killed, there succeeded him one who was a little harsher. I was very eager to see the end of his dominion also, and we began to have a third ruler still more harsh—that was you. So if you should be taken away, a worse would succeed in your place."[6]

[45] If the excess of tyranny is unbearable, some have been of the opinion that it would be an act of virtue for strong men to slay the tyrant and to expose themselves to the danger of death in order to set the multitude free.[7] An example of this occurs even in the Old Testament, for a certain Aioth slew Eglon, King of Moab, who was oppressing the people of God under

---

[6] VALERIUS MAXIMUS VI, 2, Ext. 2 (VINCENT OF BEAUVAIS, *Speculum Historiale* III, 73).

[7] Cf. JOHN OF SALISBURY, *Policraticus* VIII, 18 (788c) - 20 (797a).

harsh slavery, thrusting a dagger into his thigh; and
he was made a judge of the people.[8]

[46] But this opinion is not in accord with apostolic
teaching. For Peter admonishes us to be reverently
subject to our masters, not only to the good and gentle
but also the froward: "For if one who suffers unjustly
bear his trouble for conscience' sake, this is grace."[9]
Wherefore, when many emperors of the Romans tyran-
nically persecuted the faith of Christ, a great number
both of the nobility and the common people were con-
verted to the faith and were praised for patiently bear-
ing death for Christ. They did not resist although they
were armed, and this is plainly manifested in the case
of the holy Theban legion.[10] Aioth, then, must be
considered rather as having slain a foe than assassi-
nated a ruler, however tyrannical, of the people. Hence
in the Old Testament we also read that they who killed
Joas, the king of Juda, who had fallen away from the
worship of God, were slain and their children spared
according to the precept of the law.[11]

[47] Should private persons attempt on their own
private presumption to kill the rulers, even though
tyrants, this would be dangerous for the multitude as
well as for their rulers. This is because the wicked
usually expose themselves to dangers of this kind
more than the good, for the rule of a king, no less than
that of a tyrant, is burdensome to them since, according
to the words of Solomon:[12] "A wise king scattereth the
wicked." Consequently, by presumption of this kind,
danger to the people from the loss of a good king would

---

[8] *Judges* iii, 14 ff. See JOHN OF SALISBURY, *Policraticus* VIII, 20 (794b).
[9] I *Petr.* li, 18, 19.
[10] *Acta Sanctorum Septembris*, t. VI, 308 ff.
[11] IV *Kings* xiv, 5-6.
[12] *Prov.* xx, 26.

be more probable than relief through the removal of a tyrant.

[48] Furthermore, it seems that to proceed against the cruelty of tyrants is an action to be undertaken, not through the private presumption of a few, but rather by public authority.

[49] If to provide itself with a king belongs to the right of a given multitude, it is not unjust that the king be deposed or have his power restricted by that same multitude if, becoming a tyrant, he abuses the royal power. It must not be thought that such a multitude is acting unfaithfully in deposing the tyrant, even though it had previously subjected itself to him in perpetuity, because he himself has deserved that the covenant with his subjects should not be kept, since, in ruling the multitude, he did not act faithfully as the office of a king demands. Thus did the Romans,[13] who had accepted Tarquin the Proud as their king, cast him out from the kingship on account of his tyranny and the tyranny of his sons; and they set up in their place a lesser power, namely, the consular power. Similarly[14] Domitian, who had succeeded those most moderate emperors, Vespasian, his father, and Titus, his brother, was slain by the Roman senate when he exercised tyranny, and all his wicked deeds were justly and profitably declared null and void by a decree of the senate. Thus it came about that Blessed John the Evangelist, the beloved disciple of God, who had been exiled to the island of Patmos by that very Domitian, was sent back to Ephesus by a decree of the senate.

[13] EUSEBIUS, *Chronicorum Lib.* II: PG 19, 467a, 471b; ST. AUGUSTINE, *De Civitate Dei* V, 12.
[14] EUSEBIUS, *Chronicorum Lib.* II: PG 19, 551h; ST. JEROME, *De viris illustribus* I, 9: PL 23, 655. See also ST. AUGUSTINE, *De Civitate Dei* V, 21.

[50] If, on the other hand, it pertains to the right of a higher authority to provide a king for a certain multitude, a remedy against the wickedness of a tyrant is to be looked for from him. Thus when Archelaus, who had already begun to reign in Judaea in the place of Herod his father, was imitating his father's wickedness, a complaint against him having been laid before Caesar Augustus by the Jews, his power was at first diminished by depriving him of his title of king and by dividing one-half of his kingdom between his two brothers. Later, since he was not restrained from tyranny even by this means, Tiberius Caesar sent him into exile to Lugdunum, a city in Gaul.[15]

[51] Should no human aid whatsoever against a tyrant be forthcoming, recourse must be had to God, the King of all, Who is a helper in due time in tribulation.[16] For it lies in his power to turn the cruel heart of the tyrant to mildness.[17] According to Solomon:[18] "The heart of the king is in the hand of the Lord, withersoever He will He shall turn it." He it was who turned into mildness the cruelty of King Assuerus, who was preparing death for the Jews.[19] He it was who so filled the cruel king Nabuchodonosor with piety that he became a proclaimer of the divine power. "Therefore," he said,[20] "I, Nabuchodonosor do now praise and magnify and glorify the King of Heaven;

[15] FLAVIUS IOSEPHUS, De Bello Iud. II, 80 ff, 93, 111. ARCHELAUS, however, was not exiled to Lugdunum (Lyons) by TIBERIUS, but to "Vienna (Vienne), a town in Gaul" by AUGUSTUS (IOSEPHUS, op. cit. 111: EUSEBIUS, Chronicorum Lib. II: PG 19, 531 n: PETER COMESTOR, Historia Scholastica, In Ev. XXIV: PL 198, 1550; VINCENT OF BEAUVAIS, Spec. Hist. VI, 103.) St. Thomas was probably misled by the Glossa Ordinaria, In Matth. ii, 22: PL 114, 78. The above statement, however, is somewhat puzzling in view of what Aquinas has said in Catena Aurea, In Matth. II, 10: p. 39b, and in the commentary to St. Matthew, II, 4: p. 41b.
[16] Psalm ix, 10.   [17] Cf. Esther xv, 11.   [18] Prov. xxi, 1.
[19] See the Book of Esther.   [20] Dan. iv, 34.

because all His works are true and His ways judgments,
and they that walk in pride He is able to abase." Those
tyrants, however, whom he deems unworthy of con-
version, he is able to put out of the way or to degrade,
according to the words of the Wise Man:[21] "God hath
overturned the thrones of proud princes and hath set
up the meek in their stead." He it was who, seeing the
affliction of his people in Egypt and hearing their cry,
hurled Pharaoh, a tyrant over God's people, with all
his army into the sea.[22] He it was who not only ban-
ished from his kingly throne the above-mentioned
Nabuchodonosor because of his former pride, but also
cast him from the fellowship of men and changed him
into the likeness of a beast.[23] Indeed, his hand is not
shortened that He cannot free His people from tyrants.[24] For by Isaias[25] He promised to give his people
rest from their labours and lashings and harsh slavery
in which they had formerly served; and by Ezechiel[26]
He says: "I will deliver my flock from their mouth,"
i.e. from the mouth of shepherds who feed themselves.

[52] But to deserve to secure this benefit from God,
the people must desist from sin, for it is by divine
permission that wicked men receive power to rule as
a punishment for sin,[27] as the Lord says by the Prophet
Osee:[28] "I will give thee a king in my wrath" and it is
said in Job[29] that he "maketh a man that is a hypocrite
to reign for the sins of the people." Sin must therefore be done away with in order that the scourge of
tyrants may cease.

[21] Eccli. x, 17.   [22] Exod. xiv, 23-28.   [23] Dan. iv, 30.
[24] Isaias lix, 1.   [25] xiv, 3.   [26] xxxiv, 10.
[27] St. Gregory, Moralium L. 25, 16: PL 76, 344; St. Isidore, Sententiae 3,
48, 11: PL 83, 720. — 2 Sent., 33, I, 2 ad 5; Summa II-II, 108, 4 ad 1.
[28] xiii, 11.   [29] xxxiv, 30.

CHAPTER VII

THAT MUNDANE HONOUR AND GLORY ARE NOT AN ADEQUATE REWARD FOR A KING

[53] Since, according to what has been said thus far,[1] it is the king's duty to seek the good of the multitude, the task of a king may seem too burdensome unless some advantage to himself should result from it. It is fitting therefore to consider wherein a suitable reward for a good king is to be found.

[54] By some men this reward was considered to be nothing other than honour and glory. Whence TULLIUS says in the book *On the Republic*:[2] "The prince of the city should be nourished by glory," and ARISTOTLE seems to assign the reason for this in his *Book on Ethics*:[3] "because the prince for whom honour and glory is not sufficient consequently turns into a tyrant." For it is in the hearts of all men to seek their proper good. Therefore, if the prince is not content with glory and honour, he will seek pleasures and riches and so will resort to plundering and injuring his subjects.

[55] However, if we accept this opinion a great many incongruous results follow. In the first place, it would be costly to kings if so many labours and anxieties were to be endured for a reward so perishable, for nothing, it seems, is more perishable among human things than the glory and honour of men's favour, since it depends upon the report of men and their opinions, than which nothing in human life is more

[1]See Introduction p. xvi.
[2] ST. AUGUSTINE, *De Civ. Dei* V, 13 (CICERO, *De Republica* V, 7, 9).
[3] V, 10: 1134b 7. *In Eth.* V, 11: 1011.

fickle. And this is why the Prophet Isaias[4] calls such glory "the flower of grass."

[56] Moreover, the desire for human glory takes away greatness of soul. For he who seeks the favour of men must serve their will in all he says and does, and thus, while striving to please all, he becomes a slave to each one. Wherefore the same TULLIUS says in his book *On Duties*[5] that "the inordinate desire for glory is to be guarded against; it takes away freedom of soul, for the sake of which high-minded men should put forth all their efforts." Indeed there is nothing more becoming to a prince who has been set up for the doing of good works than greatness of soul. Thus, the reward of human glory is not enough for the services of a king.

[57] At the same time it also hurts the multitude if such a reward be set up for princes, for it is the duty of a good man to take no account of glory, just as he should take no account of other temporal goods. It is the mark of a virtuous and brave soul to despise glory as he despises life, for justice' sake: whence the strange thing results that glory ensues from virtuous acts, and out of virtue glory itself is despised: and therefore, through his very contempt for glory, a man is made glorious—according to the sentence of Fabius:[6] "He who scorns glory shall have true glory," and as SALLUST[7] says of Cato: "The less he sought glory the more he achieved it." Even the disciples of Christ "exhibited themselves as the ministers of God in

---

[4] xl, 6.   [5] *De Officiis* I, 20, 68.

[6] LIVY XXII, 39, 20. The immediate source of this "sentence" is perhaps one of the many *"Florilegia"* which were so popular in the Middle Ages.

[7] *Bellum Catilinae* 54, 6; ST. AUGUSTINE, *De Civ. Dei* V, 12.

honour and dishonour, in evil report and good report."[8] Glory is, therefore, not a fitting reward for a good man; good men spurn it. And, if it alone be set up as the reward for princes, it will follow that good men will not take upon themselves the chief office of the city, or if they take it, they will go unrewarded.

[58] Furthermore, dangerous evils come from the desire for glory. Many have been led unrestrainedly to seek glory in warfare, and have sent their armies and themselves to destruction, while the freedom of their country was turned into servitude under an enemy. Consider Torquatus, the Roman chief. In order to impress upon the people how imperative it is to avoid such danger, "he slew his own son who, being challenged by an enemy, had, through youthful impetuosity, fought and vanquished him. Yet he had done so contrary to orders given him by his father. Torquatus acted thus, lest more harm should accrue from the example of his son's presumption than advantage from the glory of slaying the enemy."[9]

[59] Moreover, the desire for glory has another vice akin to it, namely, hypocrisy. Since it is difficult to acquire true virtues, to which alone honour and glory are due, and it is therefore the lot of but a few to attain them, many who desire glory become simulators of virtue. On this account, as SALLUST[10] says: "Ambition drives many mortals to become false. They keep one thing shut up in their heart, another ready on the tongue, and they have more countenance than character." But our Saviour also calls those persons hypocrites, or simulators, who do good works that they may be seen by men.[11] Therefore, just as there is

8 II Cor. vi, 8.
10 Bellum Catilinae 10, 5.
9 St. Augustine, De Civ. Dei V, 18
11 Mt. vi, 5.

danger for the multitude, if the prince seek pleasures and riches as his reward, that he become a plunderer and abusive, so there is danger, if glory be assigned to him as reward, that he become presumptuous and a hypocrite.

[60] Looking at what the above-mentioned wise men intended to say, they do not seem to have decided upon honour and glory as the reward of a prince because they judged that the king's intention should be principally directed to that object, but because it is more tolerable for him to seek glory than to desire money or pursue pleasure. For this vice is akin to virtue inasmuch as the glory which men desire, as AUGUSTINE[12] says, is nothing else than the judgment of men who think well of men. So the desire for glory has some trace of virtue in it, at least so long as it seeks the approval of good men and is reluctant to displease them. Therefore, since few men reach true virtue, it seems more tolerable if one be set up to rule who, fearing the judgment of men, is restrained from manifest evils. For the man[13] who desires glory either endeavours to win the approval of men in the true way, by deeds of virtue, or at least strives for this by fraud and deceit. But if the one who desires to domineer lacks the desire for glory, he will have no fear of offending men of good judgment and will commonly strive to obtain what he chooses by the most open crimes. Thus he will surpass the beasts in the vices of cruelty and lust, as is evidenced in the case of the Emperor Nero, who was so effete, as AUGUSTINE[14] says, "that he despised everything virile, and yet so

[12] De Civitate Dei V, 12.
[13] This and the following propositions are owed to ST. AUGUSTINE, De Civitate Dei V, 19.　　　[14] loc. cit.

cruel that nobody would have thought him to be
effeminate." Indeed all this is quite clearly contained
in what ARISTOTLE says in his *Ethics*[15] regarding the
magnanimous man: True, he does seek honour and
glory, but not as something great which could be a
sufficient reward of virtue. And beyond this he demands nothing more of men, for among all earthly
goods the chief good, it seems, is this, that men bear
testimony to the virtue of a man.

CHAPTER VIII

THAT THE KING SHOULD LOOK TO GOD FOR ADEQUATE REWARD

[61] Therefore, since worldly honour and human
glory are not a sufficient reward for royal cares, it
remains to inquire what sort of reward is sufficient.

[62] It is proper that a king look to God for his
reward, for a servant looks to his master for the reward
of his service. The king is indeed the minister of God
in governing the people, as the Apostle[1] says: "All
power is from the Lord God" and God's minister is
"an avenger to execute wrath upon him that doth
evil." And in the *Book of Wisdom*,[2] kings are described
as being ministers of God. Consequently, kings ought
to look to God for the reward of their ruling. Now
God sometimes rewards kings for their service by
temporal goods, but such rewards are common to both
the good and the wicked. Wherefore the Lord says to
Ezechiel:[3] "Nabuchodonosor, king of Babylon, hath
made his army to undergo hard service against Tyre,
and there hath been no reward given him nor his army

---

[15] IV, 7: 1124a 16; *In Eth.* IV, 9: 755.
[1] *Rom.* xiii, 1, 4.   [2] vi, 5.   [3] xxix, 18.

for Tyre, for the service he rendered Me against it,"
for that service namely, by which, according to the
Apostle,[4] power is "the minister of God and the avenger
to execute wrath upon him that doth evil." Afterwards[5] He adds, regarding the reward: "Therefore,
thus saith the Lord God, 'I will set Nabuchodonosor
the king of Babylon in the land of Egypt, and he shall
rifle the spoils thereof, and it shall be wages for his
army.' " Therefore, if God recompenses wicked kings
who fight against the enemies of God, though not with
the intention of serving Him but to execute their own
hatred and cupidity, by giving them such great rewards as to yield them victory over their foes, subject
kingdoms to their sway and grant them spoils to rifle,
what will He do for kings who rule the people of God
and assail His enemies from a holy motive? He
promises them not an earthly reward indeed but an
everlasting one and in none other than in Himself. As
Peter[6] says to the shepherds of the people: "Feed the
flock of God that is among you and when the prince
of pastors shall appear (i.e. the King of kings, Christ)
you shall receive a never-fading crown of glory," concerning which Isaias[7] says: "The Lord shall be a crown
of glory and a garland of joy to His people."

[63] This is also clearly shown by reason. It is
implanted in the minds of all who have the use of
reason that the reward of virtue is happiness. The
virtue of anything whatsoever is explained[8] to be that
which makes its possessor good and renders his deed
good. Moreover, everyone strives by working well
to attain that which is most deeply implanted in desire,

[4] *Rom.* xiii, 4. [5] *Ezech.* xxix, 19.
[6] I *Petr.* v, 2, 4. [7] xxviii, 5.
[8] *Eth. Nic.* II, 6: 1106a 15. *In Eth.* II, 6: 307 f; *Summa* I-II, 55, 3.

namely, to be happy.[9] This, no one is able not to wish.
It is therefore fitting to expect as a reward for virtue
that which makes man happy. Now, if to work well
is a virtuous deed, and the king's work is to rule his
people well, then that which makes him happy will
be the king's reward. What this is has now to be
considered.[10] Happiness, we say, is the ultimate end
of our desires. Now the movement of desire does not
go on to infinity else natural desire would be vain,
for infinity cannot be traversed. Since, then, the desire
of an intellectual nature is for universal good, that
good alone can make it truly happy which, when
attained, leaves no further good to be desired. Whence
happiness is called the perfect good[11] inasmuch as it
comprises in itself all things desirable. But no earthly
good is such a good. They who have riches desire to
have more, they who enjoy pleasure desire to enjoy
more, and the like is clear for the rest: and if they do
not seek more, they at least desire that those they have
should abide or that others should follow in their
stead. For nothing permanent is found in earthly
things. Consequently there is nothing earthly which
can calm desire. Thus, nothing earthly can make man
happy, so that it may be a fitting reward for a king.

[64] Again, the last perfection and perfect good of
anything one chooses depends upon something higher,
for even bodily things are made better by the addition
of better things and worse by being mixed with baser
things. If gold is mingled with silver, the silver is
made better, while by an admixture of lead it is rendered impure. Now it is manifest that all earthly

[9] *Summa* I-II, 1, 6, 7.
[10] On what follows in this chapter cf. *CG* III, 27-37; *Summa* I-II, 2.
[11] *Eth. Nic.* I, 1: 1094a 22.

things are beneath the human mind. But happiness is the last perfection and the perfect good of man, which all men desire to reach. Therefore there is no earthly thing which could make man happy, nor is any earthly thing a sufficient reward for a king. For, as AUGUSTINE[12] says, "we do not call Christian princes happy merely because they have reigned a long time, or because after a peaceful death they have left their sons to rule, or because they subdued the enemies of the state, or because they were able to guard against or to suppress citizens who rose up against them. Rather do we call them happy if they rule justly, if they prefer to rule their passions rather than nations, and if they do all things not for the love of vainglory but for the love of eternal happiness. Such Christian emperors we say are happy, now in hope, afterwards in very fact when that which we await shall come to pass." But neither is there any other created thing which would make a man happy and which could be set up as the reward for a king. For the desire of each thing tends towards its source, whence is the cause of its being. But the cause of the human soul is none other than God Who made it to His own image. Therefore it is God alone Who can still the desires of man and make him happy and be the fitting reward for a king.

[65] Furthermore, the human mind knows the universal good through the intellect, and desires it through the will: but the universal good is not found except in God. Therefore there is nothing which could make man happy, fulfilling his every desire, but God, of Whom it is said in the Psalm:[13] "Who satisfieth thy desire with good things." In this, therefore, should the

---

[12] *De Civitate Dei* V, 24.
[13] cii, 5.

king place his reward. Wherefore, King David,[14] with this in mind, said: "What have I in heaven? And besides Thee what do I desire upon earth?" and he afterwards adds in answer to this question: "It is good for me to adhere to my God and to put my hope in the Lord God." For it is He Who gives salvation to kings, not merely temporal salvation by which He saves both men and beasts together, but also that salvation of which He says by the mouth of Isaias:[15] "But my salvation shall be for ever," that salvation by which He saves man and makes them equal to the angels.

[66] It can thus also be verified that the reward of the king is honour and glory. What worldly and frail honour can indeed be likened to this honour that a man be made a "citizen with the Saints and a kinsman of God,"[16] numbered among the sons of God, and that he obtain the inheritance of the heavenly kingdom with Christ? This is the honour of which King David,[17] in desire and wonder, says: "Thy friends, O God, are made exceedingly honourable." And further, what glory of human praise can be compared to this, not uttered by the false tongue of flatterers nor the fallacious opinion of men, but issuing from the witness of our inmost conscience and confirmed by the testimony of God, Who promises to those who confess Him that He will confess them before the Angels of God in the glory of the Father?[18] They who seek this glory will find it and they will win the glory of men which they do not seek: witness Solomon, who not only received from the Lord wisdom which he sought, but was made glorious above other kings.[19]

[14] *Psalm* lxxii 25, 28. [15] li, 6. [16] *Eph.* ii, 19.
[17] cxxxviii, 17. [18] *Mt.* x, 32. [19] III *Kings* x, 23.

CHAPTER IX

WHAT DEGREE OF HEAVENLY BEATITUDE THE KING MAY OBTAIN

[67] Now it remains further to consider that they who discharge the kingly office worthily and laudably will obtain an elevated and outstanding degree of heavenly happiness.

[68] For if happiness is the reward of virtue, it follows that a higher degree of happiness is due to greater virtue. Now, that indeed is signal virtue by which a man can guide not only himself but others, and the more persons he rules the greater his virtue.[1] Similarly, in regard to bodily strength, a man is reputed to be more powerful the more adversaries he can beat or the more weights he can lift. Thus, greater virtue is required to rule a household than to rule one's self, and much greater to rule a city and a kingdom. To discharge well the office of a king is therefore a work of extraordinary virtue. To it, therefore, is due an extraordinary reward of happiness.

[69] Again, those who rule others well are more worthy of praise than those who act well under others' direction. This applies to the field of all arts and sciences.[2] In the speculative sciences, for instance, it is nobler to impart truth to others by teaching than to be able to grasp what is taught by others. So, too, in matters of the crafts, an architect who plans a building is more highly esteemed and paid a higher wage than

[1] ARISTOTLE, *Eth. Nic.* V, 3: 1129b 31 ff; *Rhetorics* I, 9: 1366b 3; DIONYSIUS, *De Caelesti Hierarchia* 2: PG 3, 165B. *In Eth.* V, 2: 910. For other texts of St. Thomas see ESCHMANN, *Glossary* 142 ff.
[2] ARISTOTLE, *Eth. Nic.* I, 1: 1094a 9; *Metaph.* I, 1: 987a 30; *Phys,* II, 10: 194a 36. 3 *Sent.*, 35, I, 4, 1 *in* 3; *Summa* I-II, 15, 4 *ad* 1.

is the builder who does the manual labour under his direction; also, in warfare the strategy of the general wins greater glory from victory than the bravery of the soldier. Now the ruler of a multitude stands in the same relation to the virtuous deeds performed by each individual as the teacher to the matters taught, the architect to the buildings, and the general to the wars. Consequently, the king is worthy of a greater reward if he governs his subjects well than any of his subjects who act well under him.

[70] Further, if it is the part of virtue to render a man's work good, it is, it seems, from greater virtue that one does greater good. But the good of the multitude is greater and more divine than the good of one man.[3] Wherefore the evil of one man is sometimes endured if it redounds to the good of the multitude, as when a robber is killed to bring peace to the multitude.[4] God Himself would not allow evils to be in the world were it not for the fact that He brings good out of them for the advantage and beauty of the universe.[5] Now it belongs to the office of the king to have zealous concern for the good of the multitude. Therefore a greater reward is due to the king for good ruling than to the subject for acting according to rule.

[71] This will become clearer if considered in greater detail. For a private person is praised by men, and his deed reckoned for reward by God, if he helps the needy, brings peace to those in discord, rescues one oppressed by a mightier; in a word, if in any way he gives to another assistance or advice for his welfare. How much the more, then, is he to be praised by men and rewarded by God who makes a whole province

[3] ARISTOTLE, Eth. Nic. I, 2: 1094b 7. In Eth. I, 2: 30.
[4] Cf. Summa I-II, 19, 10 et alibi. [5] CG III, 71; ibid. 46, et alibi.

rejoice in peace, who restrains violence, preserves justice and arranges by his laws and precepts what is to be done by men?

[72] The greatness of kingly virtue also appears in this, that he bears a special likeness to God, since he does in his kingdom what God does in the world;[6] wherefore in *Exodus*[7] the judges of the people are called gods, and also among the Romans the emperors received the appellative *Divus*.[8] Now the more a thing approaches to the likeness of God the more acceptable it is to Him. Hence, also, the Apostle[9] urges: "Be ye therefore imitators of God as most dear children." But if according to the saying of the Wise Man,[10] every beast loveth its like inasmuch as causes bear some likeness to the caused, it follows that good kings are most pleasing to God and are to be most highly rewarded by Him.

[73] Likewise, if I may use the words of GREGORY:[11] "What else is it (for a king) to be at the pinnacle of power if not to find himself in a mental storm? When the sea is calm even an inexperienced man can steer a ship straight; when the sea is troubled by stormy waves, even an experienced sailor is bewildered. Whence it frequently happens that in the business of government the practice of good works is lost which

---

[6] That "the king stands to the State in the same relation as God to the world" (STOBAEUS IV, 7, 61: IV, 263, 7) is a characteristic doctrine of Hellenistic political philosophy due to Oriental as well as Pythagorean-Platonic conceptions. Among the Latins this teaching was preserved and transmitted by authors such as the AMBROSIASTER (PL 35, 2236: *Dei enim imaginem habet rex*), JOHN OF SALISBURY (*Policraticus* VIII, 17: 778a: *Imago quaedam divinitatis est princeps*), and others. See GOODENOUGH 68 ff, 74, 100; BERGES 26 ff.

[7] xxii, 9.

[8] See above note 6. *Exp. in L. De Causis* 3: I, 208; *Summa* II-II, 99, 1 *ad* 1.

[9] *Eph.* v, 1.   [10] *Eccli.* xiii, 9.

[11] *Regula Pastoralis* I, 9: PL 77, 22B.

in tranquil times was maintained." For, as AUGUSTINE[12] says, it is very difficult for rulers "not to be puffed up amid flattering and honouring tongues and the obsequiousness of those who bow too humbly, but to remember that they are men." It is said also in *Ecclesiasticus*:[13] "Blessed is the rich man that hath not gone after gold nor put his trust in money nor in treasures, and that could have transgressed with impunity and hath not transgressed and could do evil things and hath not done them." Wherefore, having been tried in the work of virtue, he is found faithful and so, according to the proverb of Bias:[14] "Authority shows the man." For many who seemed virtuous while they were in lowly state fall from virtue when they reach the pinnacle of power. The very difficulty, then, of acting well, which besets kings, makes them more worthy of greater reward; and if through weakness they sometimes do amiss, they are rendered more excusable before men and more easily obtain forgiveness from God provided, as AUGUSTINE[15] says, they do not neglect to offer up to their true God the sacrifice of humility, mercy, and prayer for their sins. As an example of this, the Lord said to Elias concerning Achab, king of Israel, who had sinned a great deal:[16] "Because he hath humbled himself for My sake, I will not bring the evil in his days."

[74] That a very high reward is due to kings is not only demonstrated by reason but is also confirmed by divine authority. It is said in the prophecy of Zacharias[17] that, in that day of blessedness wherein God will be the protector of the inhabitants of Jerusalem (*i.e.*

---

[12] *De Civitate Dei* V, 24.
[14] ARISTOTLE, *Eth. Nic.* V, 3: 1130a 1.
[16] III *Kings* xxi, 29.
[13] xxxi, 8, 10.
[15] *De Civitate Dei* V, 24.
[17] xii, 8.

in the vision of eternal peace), the houses of others will be as the house of David, because all will then be kings and reign with Christ as the members with their head. But the house of David will be as the house of God, because just as he carried out the work of God among the people by ruling faithfully, so in his reward he will adhere more closely to God. Likewise, among the Gentiles this was dimly realized, as in a dream, for they thought to transform into gods the rulers and preservers of their cities.[18]

CHAPTER X

What Advantages Which Are Rendered to Kings Are Lost by the Tyrant

[75] Since such a magnificent reward in heavenly blessedness is in store for kings who have acted well in ruling, they ought to keep careful watch over themselves in order not to turn to tyranny. Nothing, indeed, can be more acceptable to them than to be transferred from the royal honour, to which they are raised on earth, into the glory of the heavenly kingdom. Tyrants, on the contrary, who desert justice for a few earthly advantages, are deprived of such a great reward which they could have obtained by ruling justly. How foolish it is to sacrifice the greatest and eternal goods for trifling, temporal goods is clear to everyone but a fool or an infidel.

[18] See P. Wendland 143 ff.

[76] It is to be added further, however, that the very temporal advantages for which tyrants abandon justice work to the greater profit of kings when they observe justice.

[77] First of all, among all worldly things there is nothing which seems worthy to be preferred to friendship. Friendship unites good men and preserves and promotes virtue. Friendship is needed by all men in whatsoever occupations they engage. In prosperity it does not thrust itself unwanted upon us, nor does it desert us in adversity. It is what brings with it the greatest delight, to such an extent that all that pleases is changed to weariness when friends are absent, and all difficult things are made easy and as nothing by love. There is no tyrant so cruel that friendship does not bring him pleasure. When Dionysius,[1] sometime tyrant of Syracuse, wanted to kill one of two friends, Damon and Pythias, the one who was to be killed asked leave to go home and set his affairs in order, and the other friend surrendered himself to the tyrant as security for his return. When the appointed day was approaching and he had not yet returned, everyone said that his hostage was a fool, but he declared he had no fear whatever regarding his friend's loyalty. The very hour when he was to be put to death, his friend returned. Admiring the courage of both, the tyrant remitted the sentence on account of the loyalty of their friendship, and asked in addition that they should receive him as a third member in their bond of friendship.

[78] Yet, although tyrants desire this very benefit of friendship, they cannot obtain it, for when they

---

[1] VALERIUS MAXIMUS IV, 7, Ext. 1; VINCENT OF BEAUVAIS, Specul. Doctrinale V, 84.

seek their own good instead of the common good there
is little or no communion between them and their
subjects. Now all friendship is concluded upon the
basis of something common among those who are to
be friends,[2] for we see that those are united in friendship who have in common either their natural origin,
or some similarity in habits of life, or any kind of
social interests. Consequently there can be little or
no friendship between tyrants and their subjects.
When the latter are oppressed by tyrannical injustice
and feel they are not loved but despised, they certainly
do not conceive any love, for it is too great a virtue
for the common man to love his enemies and to do
good to his persecutors. Nor have tyrants any reason
to complain of their subjects if they are not loved by
them, since they do not act towards them in such a
way that they ought to be loved by them. Good kings,
on the contrary, are loved by many when they show
that they love their subjects and are studiously intent
on the common welfare, and when their subjects can
see that they derive many benefits from this zealous
care. For to hate their friends and return evil for
good to their benefactors—this, surely, would be too
great a malice to ascribe fittingly to the generality of
men.

[79] The consequence of this love is that the government of good kings is stable, because their subjects do
not refuse to expose themselves to any danger whatsoever on behalf of such kings. An example of this
is to be seen in Julius Caesar who, as Suetonius[3] relates, loved his soldiers to such an extent that when

[2] Cf. Aristotle, Eth. Nic. VIII, 12: 1161b 11. In Eth. VIII, 12:1702 ff;
3 Sent., 29, 6: De Perfectione XIII; Summa II-II, 23, 5, et alibi.
[3] Divus Iulius 67.

he heard that some of them were slaughtered, "he refused to cut either hair or beard until he had taken vengeance." In this way, he made his soldiers most loyal to himself as well as most valiant, so that many, on being taken prisoner, refused to accept their lives when offered them on the condition that they serve against Caesar. Octavianus Augustus,[4] also, who was most moderate in his use of power, was so loved by his subjects that some of them "on their deathbeds provided in their wills a thank-offering to be paid by the immolation of animals, so grateful were they that the emperor's life outlasted their own." Therefore it is no easy task to shake the government of a prince whom the people so unanimously love. This is why Solomon[5] says: "The king that judgeth the poor in justice, his throne shall be established forever."

[80] The government of tyrants, on the other hand, cannot last long because it is hateful to the multitude, and what is against the wishes of the multitude cannot be long preserved. For a man can hardly pass through this present life without suffering some adversities, and in the time of his adversity occasion cannot be lacking to rise against the tyrant; and when there is an opportunity there will not be lacking at least one of the multitude to use it. Then the people will fervently favour the insurgent, and what is attempted with the sympathy of the multitude will not easily fail of its effects. It can thus scarcely come to pass that the government of a tyrant will endure for a long time.

[81] This is very clear, too, if we consider the means by which a tyrannical government is upheld. It is not upheld by love, since there is little or no bond of

⁴ Sᴜᴇᴛᴏɴɪᴜs, *Divus Augustus* 59.
⁵ *Prov.* xxix, 14.

friendship between the subject multitude and the tyrant, as is evident from what we have said. On the other hand, tyrants cannot rely on the loyalty of their subjects, for such a degree of virtue is not found among the generality of men, that they should be restrained by the virtue of fidelity from throwing off the yoke of unmerited servitude, if they are able to do so. Nor would it perhaps be a violation of fidelity at all, according to the opinion of many,[6] to frustrate the wickedness of tyrants by any means whatsoever. It remains, then, that the government of a tyrant is maintained by fear alone and consequently they strive with all their might to be feared by their subjects. Fear, however, is a weak support. Those who are kept down by fear will rise against their rulers if the opportunity ever occurs when they can hope to do it with impunity, and they will rebel against their rulers all the more furiously the more they have been kept in subjection against their will by fear alone, just as water confined under pressure flows with greater impetus when it finds an outlet. That very fear itself is not without danger, because many become desperate from excessive fear, and despair of safety impels a man boldly to dare anything. Therefore the government of a tyrant cannot be of long duration.

[82] This appears clearly from examples no less than from reason. If we scan the history of antiquity and the events of modern times,[7] we shall scarcely find one government of a tyrant which lasted a long time. So ARISTOTLE, in his *Politics*,[8] after enumerating

[6] For instance MANEGOLD OF LAUTENBACH, *Ad Gebhardum Liber*, p. 365; see McILWAIN 210. For other authors see CARLYLE III, 130 ff. .See above § 49, p. 27.
[7] See ch. V, note 3, p. 23. As to the "history of antiquity" see the following note.   [8] V, 12: 1315b 11-39.

many tyrants, shows that all their governments were of short duration; although some of them reigned a fairly long time because they were not very tyrannical but in many things imitated the moderation of kings. [83] All this becomes still more evident if we consider the divine judgment, for, as we read in Job,[9] "He maketh a man who is a hypocrite to reign for the sins of the people." No one, indeed, can be more truly called a hypocrite than the man who assumes the office of king and acts like a tyrant, for a hypocrite is one who mimics the person of another, as is done on the stage. Hence God permits tyrants to get into power to punish the sins of the subjects. In Holy Scripture it is customary to call such punishment the anger of God. Thus in Osee[10] the Lord says: "I will give thee a king in my wrath." Unhappy is a king who is given to the people in God's wrath, for his power cannot be stable, because "God forgets not to show mercy nor does He shut up His mercies in His anger."[11] On the contrary, as we read in Joel:[12] "He is patient and rich in mercy and ready to repent of the evil." So God does not permit tyrants to reign a long time, but after the storm brought on the people through these tyrants, He restores transquillity by casting them down. Therefore the Wise Man[13] says: "God has overturned the thrones of proud princes and hath set up the meek in their stead."

[84] Experience further shows that kings acquire more wealth through justice than tyrants do through rapine. Because[14] the government of tyrants is displeasing to the multitude subject to it, tyrants must

---

[9]xxiv, 30. Cf. above § 52, p. 29.   [10]xiii, 11.
[11]Psalm lxxvi, 10.   [12]ii, 13.   [13]Eccli. x, 17.
[14] On the following cf. ARISTOTLE, Pol. III, 14: 1285a 24-29.

have a great many satellites to safeguard themselves
against their subjects. On these it is necessary to spend
more than they can rob from their subjects. On the
contrary, the government of kings, since it is pleasing
to their subjects, has for its protection, instead of hire-
lings, all the subjects. And they demand no pay but,
in time of need, freely give to their kings more than
the tyrants can take. Thus the words of Solomon[15]
are fulfilled: "Some (namely, the kings) distribute
their own goods (doing good to their subjects) and
grow richer; others (namely, the tyrants) take away
what is not their own and are always in want." In the
same way it comes to pass, by the just judgment of
God, that those who unjustly heap up riches, uselessly
scatter them or are justly deprived of them. For, as
Solomon[16] says: "A covetous man shall not be satisfied
with money and he that loveth riches shall reap no
fruit from them." Nay, more, we read in *Proverbs*:[17]
"He that is greedy of gain troubleth his own house."
But to kings who seek justice, God gives wealth, as
He did to Solomon who, when he sought wisdom to do
justice, received a promise of an abundance of wealth.[18]

[85] It seems superfluous to speak about fame, for
who can doubt that good kings live in a sense in the
praises of men, not only in this life, but still more, after
their death, and that men yearn for them? But the
name of wicked kings straightway vanishes or, if they
have been excessive in their wickedness, they are remembered with execration. Thus Solomon[19] says:
"The memory of the just is with praises, and the name
of the wicked shall rot," either because it vanishes or
it remains with stench.

[15] *Prov. xi*, 24.   [16] *Eccles.* v, 9.   [17] xv, 27.
[18] II *Paralip.* i, 10-12.   [19] *Prov.* x, 7.

CHAPTER XI

What Punishments Are in Store for a Tyrant

[86] From the above arguments[1] it is evident that stability of power, wealth, honour and fame come to fulfil the desires of kings rather than tyrants, and it is in seeking to acquire these things unduly that princes turn to tyranny. For no one falls away from justice except through a desire for some temporal advantage.

[87] The tyrant, moreover, loses the surpassing beatitude which is due as a reward to kings and, which is still more serious, brings upon himself great suffering as a punishment. For if the man who despoils a single man, or casts him into slavery, or kills him, deserves the greatest punishment (death in the judgment of men, and in the judgment of God eternal damnation), how much worse tortures must we consider a tyrant deserves, who on all sides robs everybody, works against the common liberty of all, and kills whom he will at his merest whim?

[88] Again, such men rarely repent; but puffed up by the wind of pride, deservedly abandoned by God for their sins, and besmirched by the flattery of men, they can rarely make worthy satisfaction. When will they ever restore all those things which they have received beyond their just due? Yet no one doubts that they are bound to restore those ill-gotten goods. When will they make amends to those whom they have oppressed and unjustly injured in their many ways?

[89] The malice of their impenitence is increased by the fact that they consider everything licit which they can do unresisted and with impunity. Hence they not

[1] Ch. X.

only make no effort to repair the evil they have done but, taking their customary way of acting as their authority, they hand on their boldness in sinning to posterity. Consequently they are held guilty before God, not only for their own sins, but also for the crimes of those to whom they gave the occasion of sin.

[90] Their sin is made greater also from the dignity of the office they have assumed. Just as an earthly king inflicts a heavier punishment upon his ministers if he finds them traitors to him, so God will punish more severely those whom He made the executors and ministers of His government if they act wickedly, turning God's judgment into bitterness. Hence, in the *Book of Wisdom*,[2] the following words are addressed to wicked kings: "Because being ministers of His kingdom, you have not judged rightly nor kept the law of justice nor walked according to the will of God, horribly and speedily will He appear to you, for a most severe judgment shall be for them that bear rule; for to him that is little, mercy is granted, but the mighty shall be mightily tormented." And to Nabuchodonosor it is said by Isaias:[3] "But yet thou shalt be brought down to hell, into the depth of the pit. They that shall see thee shall turn toward thee and behold thee" as one more deeply buried in punishments.

[2] vi, 5-7.
[3] xiv, 15-16.

CHAPTER XII (I, 11)

SUMMARY OF THIS FIRST BOOK

[91] So,[1] then, if to kings an abundance of temporal goods is given and an eminent degree of beatitude prepared for them by God, while tyrants are often prevented from obtaining even the temporal goods which they covet, subjected also to many dangers and, worse still, deprived of eternal happiness and destined for most grievous punishment, surely those who undertake the office of ruling must earnestly strive to act as kings towards their subjects, and not as tyrants.

[92] What has been said hitherto should suffice in order to show what a king is, and that it is good for the multitude to have a king, and also that it is expedient for a ruler to conduct himself towards the multitude of his subjects as a king, not as a tyrant.

[1]See Introduction p. xiv.

BOOK TWO

CHAPTER I (I, 12)

ON THE DUTIES OF A KING

[93] The next point[1] to be considered is what the kingly office is and what qualities the king should have. Since things which are in accordance with art are an imitation of the things which are in accordance with nature (from which we accept the rules to act according to reason), it seems best that we learn about the kingly office from the pattern of the regime of nature.[2]

[94] In things of nature there is both a universal and a particular government. The former is God's government Whose rule embraces all things and Whose providence governs them all. The latter is found in man and it is much like the divine government. Hence man is called a *microcosmos*.[3] Indeed there is a similitude

---

[1] See Introduction p. xvi.

[2] This methodical principle should not be considered as St. Thomas' last word in the matter. The method of the *Summa* II-II, 47, 10-12 (on governmental prudence) is distinctly different. See M.-C. CHENU, *Bull. Thom.* VI, 576, n. 2.

[3] Cf. ARISTOTLE, *Phys.* VIII, 2: 252b 26; ST. GREGORY, *Homil. in Evang.* II, 29: PL 76, 1214. On the history of this notion which is found "in two different streams of thought", viz. the Neoplatonic and the Aristotelian systems, see MULLER-THYM 14 ff. "On the rare occasions where St. Thomas uses [this] formula (*In Phys.* VIII, 4; *Summa* I, 96, 2 et al.), he wishes it to be taken rather in the sense in which the providence exercised by reason over the members of the body and the use of the faculties is likened to the providence which God exercises in the world." If the idea of the *microcosm* is extended to mean that God is in the world as the soul *is* in the body, then the soul would no longer be the form of the body in the Aristotelian and Thomistic sense; rather it would be a detached substance in its own right. See *Summa* I-II, 17, 8 in 2 and *ad* 2; *ibid.* 110, 1 *ad* 2.

between both governments in regard to their form; for just as the universe of corporeal creatures and all spiritual powers come under the divine government, in like manner the members of the human body and all the powers of the soul are governed by reason. Thus, in a proportionate manner, reason is to man what God is to the world. Since, however, man is by nature a social animal living in a multitude, as we have pointed out above,[4] the analogy with the divine government is found in him not only in this way that one man governs himself by reason, but also in that the multitude of men is governed by the reason of one man. This is what first of all constitutes the office of a king. True, among certain animals that live socially there is a likeness to the king's rulership; so we say that there are kings among bees. Yet animals exercise rulership not through reason but through their natural instinct which is implanted in them by the Great Ruler, the Author of nature.

[95] Therefore let the king recognize that such is the office which he undertakes, namely, that he is to be in the kingdom what the soul is in the body, and what God is in the world.[5] If he reflect seriously upon this, a zeal for justice will be enkindled in him when he contemplates that he has been appointed to this position in place of God, to exercise judgment in his kingdom; further, he will acquire the gentleness of clemency and mildness when he considers as his own members those individuals who are subject to his rule.

[4] I, 1, § 4, p. 3.
[5] See above I, 9, n. 6, p. 41. Cf. GOODENOUGH 70.

CHAPTER II (I, 13)

What It Is Incumbent Upon a King to Do and How He Should Go About Doing It

[96] Let us then examine what God does in the world, for in this way we shall be able to see what it is incumbent upon a king to do.

[97] Looking at the world as a whole, there are two works of God to be considered: the first is creation; the second, God's government of the things created. These two works are, in like manner, performed by the soul in the body since, first, by the virtue of the soul the body is formed, and then the latter is governed and moved by the soul.[1]

[98] Of these works, the second more properly pertains to the office of kingship. Therefore government belongs to all kings (the very name *rex* is derived from the fact that they direct the government), while the first work does not fall to all kings, for not all kings establish the kingdom or city in which they rule but bestow their regal care upon a kingdom or city already established. We must remember, however, that if there were no one to establish the city or kingdom,[2] there would be no question of governing the kingdom. The very notion of kingly office, then, comprises the establishment of a city and kingdom, and some kings have indeed established cities in which to rule; for example, Ninus founded Ninevah, and Romulus, Rome. It pertains also to the governing office to pre-

[1] *In De Anima* II, 7: 318 ff; *ibid.* I, 14: 206.

[2] "Founder", "Creator", was one of the official titles of Hellenistic rulers. According to Cicero (*Pro Marcello* 27) it was Caesar's task to found the state anew and to give the world peace and quiet. Goodenough 98 f.

serve the things governed, and to use them for the
purpose for which they were established. If, therefore, one does not know how a kingdom is established,
one cannot fully understand the task of its government.
[99] Now, from the example of the creation of the
world one may learn how a kingdom is established.
In creation we may consider, first, the production of
things; secondly, the orderly distinction of the parts
of the world.³ Further, we observe that different
species of things are distributed in different parts of
the world: stars in the heavens, fowls in the air, fishes
in the water, and animals on land. We notice further
that, for each species, the things it needs are abund-
antly provided by the Divine Power. Moses has
minutely and carefully set forth this plan of how the
world was made.⁴ First of all, he sets forth the production of things in these words: "In the beginning God
created the heavens and the earth." Next, he declares
that all things were distinguished from one another by
God according to a suitable order: day from night,
higher things from lower, the sea from the dry land.
He next relates that the sky was adorned with lumi-
naries, the air with birds, the sea with fishes, the earth
with animals; finally, dominion over earth and animals
was given to men. He further states that, by Divine
Providence, plants were made for the use of men and
the other animals.
[100] Of course the founder of a city and kingdom
cannot produce anew men, places in which to dwell,
and the other necessities of life. He has to make use
of those which already exist in nature, just as the other
arts derive the material for their work from nature;

³ *Summa* I, 44, *prol.*
⁴ *Gen.* i, 1 ff.

as, for example, the smith takes iron, the builder wood and stone, to use in their respective arts. Therefore the founder of a city and kingdom must first choose a suitable place which will preserve the inhabitants by its healthfulness,[5] provide the necessities of life by its fruitfulness,[6] please them with its beauty,[7] and render them safe from their enemies by its natural protection. If any of these advantages be lacking, the place will be more or less convenient in proportion as it offers more or less of the said advantages, or the more essential of them. Next, the founder of a city and kingdom must mark out the chosen place according to the exigencies of things necessary for the perfection of the city and kingdom. For example, when a kingdom is to be founded, he will have to determine which place is suitable for establishing cities, and which is best for villages and hamlets, where to locate the places of learning, the military training camps, the markets —and so on with other things which the perfection of the kingdom requires. And if it is a question of founding a city, he will have to determine what site is to be assigned to the churches, the law courts, and the various trades.[8] Furthermore, he will have to gather together the men, who must be apportioned suitable locations according to their respective occupations. Finally, he must provide for each one what is necessary for his particular condition and state in life; otherwise, the kingdom or city could never endure.

[101] These are, briefly, the duties that pertain to the office of king in founding a city and kingdom, as derived from a comparison with the creation of the world.

[5]See below ch. V and VI, p. 68 ff.   [6]See below ch. VII, p. 74 ff.
[7]See below ch. VIII, p. 78 ff.   [8]Cf. § 14, note 22, p. 9.

CHAPTER III (I, 14)

THAT THE OFFICE OF GOVERNING THE KINGDOM SHOULD BE LEARNED FROM THE DIVINE GOVERNMENT

[102] Just as the founding of a city or kingdom may suitably be learned from the way in which the world was created, so too the way to govern may be learned from the divine government of the world.

[103] Before[1] going into that, however, we should consider that to govern is to lead the thing governed in a suitable way towards its proper end. Thus a ship is said to be governed when, through the skill of the pilot, it is brought unharmed and by a direct route to harbour. Consequently, if a thing be directed to an end outside itself[2] (as a ship to the harbour), it is the governor's duty, not only to preserve the thing unharmed, but further to guide it towards this end. If, on the contrary, there be a thing whose end is not outside itself, then the governor's endeavours will merely tend to preserve the thing undamaged in its proper perfection.

[104] Nothing of this kind is to be found in reality, except God Himself, Who is the end of all. However, as concerns the thing which is directed to an end outside itself, care is exercised by different providers in different ways. One might have the task of preserving a thing in its being, another of bringing it to a further perfection. Such is clearly the case in the example of the ship; (the first meaning of the word *gubernator* [governor] is *pilot*.) It is the carpenter's business to repair anything which might be broken, while the pilot

[1]See Introduction p. xix.
ARISTOTLE, *Metaph. Lambda* 10: 1075a 11 sqq. *In Met.* XII, 12: 2627.

bears the responsibility of bringing the ship to port. It is the same with man. The doctor sees to it that a man's life is preserved; the tradesman supplies the necessities of life; the teacher takes care that man may learn the truth; and the tutor sees that he lives according to reason.

[105] Now if man were not ordained to another end outside himself, the above-mentioned cares would be sufficient for him. But as long as man's mortal life endures there is an extrinsic good for him, namely, final beatitude which is looked for after death in the enjoyment of God, for as the Apostle[3] says: "As long as we are in the body we are far from the Lord." Consequently the Christian man, for whom that beatitude has been purchased by the blood of Christ, and who, in order to attain it, has received the earnest of the Holy Ghost, needs another and spiritual care to direct him to the harbour of eternal salvation, and this care is provided for the faithful by the ministers of the church of Christ.

[106] Now the same judgment is to be formed about the end of society as a whole as about the end of one man.[4] If, therefore, the ultimate end of man were some good that existed in himself, then the ultimate end of the multitude to be governed would likewise be for the multitude to acquire such good, and persevere in its possession. If such an ultimate end either of an individual man or a multitude were a corporeal one, namely, life and health of body, to govern would then be a physician's charge. If that ultimate end were an abundance of wealth, then knowledge of economics would have the last word in the community's govern-

³ II Cor. v, 6.
⁴ ARISTOTLE, Pol. VII, 2: 1324a 4; ibid. 3: 1325b 15, 31.

ment. If the good of the knowledge of truth were of such a kind that the multitude might attain to it, the king would have to be a teacher. It is, however, clear that the end of a multitude gathered together is to live virtuously. For men form a group for the purpose of *living well*" together, a thing which the individual man living alone could not attain, and *good life* is virtuous life. Therefore, virtuous life is the end for which men gather together. The evidence for this lies in the fact that only those who render mutual assistance to one another in living well form a genuine part of an assembled multitude. If men assembled merely to live, then animals and slaves would form a part of the civil community.⁶ Or, if men assembled only to accrue wealth, then all those who traded together would belong to one city. Yet we see that only such are regarded as forming one multitude as are directed by the same laws and the same government to live well.

[107] Yet through virtuous living man is further ordained to a higher end, which consists in the enjoyment of God, as we have said above. Consequently, since society must have the same end as the individual man, it is not the ultimate end of an assembled multitude to live virtuously, but through virtuous living to attain to the possession of God.⁷

[108] If this end could be attained by the power of human nature, then the duty of a king would have to include the direction of men to it. We are supposing,

⁵ ARISTOTLE, *Pol.* I, 2: 1252b 30; *ibid.* III, 9: 1280b 33. The source of what follows is again ARISTOTLE, *Pol.* III, 9: 1280a 25-1281a 10. Especially derived from the Stagirite are (a) the definition of "good life" which is "virtuous life" (1280b 5-10), (b) the remark about slaves and animals (1280a 32), (c) the remark that the exchange of material goods does not make a society, i.e., a state (1280a 25, b 23: ARISTOTLE'S criticism of PLATO.)

⁶ See *Summa* I-II, 98, 6 *ad* 2.　　⁷ Cf. *Summa* I-II, 6 *prol.*

of course, that he is called king to whom the supreme power of governing in human affairs is entrusted. Now the higher the end to which a government is ordained, the loftier that government is. Indeed, we always find that the one to whom it pertains to achieve the final end commands those who execute the things that are ordained to that end.[8] For example, the captain, whose business it is to regulate navigation, tells the shipbuilder what kind of ship he must construct to be suitable for navigation; and the ruler of a city, who makes use of arms, tells the blacksmith what kind of arms to make. But because a man does not attain his end, which is the possession of God, by human power but by divine—according to the words of the Apostle:[9] "By the grace of God life everlasting"—, therefore the task of leading him to that last end does not pertain to human but to divine government.

[109] Consequently, government of this kind pertains to that king who is not only a man, but also God, namely, our Lord Jesus Christ, Who by making men sons of God brought them to the glory of Heaven. This then is the government which has been delivered to Him and which "shall not be destroyed,"[10] on account of which He is called, in Holy Writ, not Priest only, but King. As Jeremias[11] says: "The king shall reign and he shall be wise." Hence a royal priesthood is derived from Him, and what is more, all those who believe in Christ, in so far as they are His members, are called kings and priests.[12]

[110] Thus, in order that spiritual things might be distinguished from earthly things,[13] the ministry of this

[8] ARISTOTLE, Eth. Nic. I, 1: 1094a 10. In Eth. I, 1: 16; CG III, 64; ibid. 76, et alibi.   [9] Rom. vi, 23.   [10] Dan. vii, 14.   [11] xxiii, 5.
[12] Apoc. i, 6; v, 10; xx, 6. Cf. Pope GELASIUS, Tomus: PL 59, 109A.
[13] GELASIUS loc. cit.; Decret. GRATIANI D. 96, c. 6.

kingdom has been entrusted not to earthly kings but to priests, and most of all to the chief priest, the successor of St. Peter, the Vicar of Christ, the Roman Pontiff. To him all the kings of the Christian People[14] are to be subject as to our Lord Jesus Christ Himself.[15] For those to whom pertains the care of intermediate ends should be subject to him to whom pertains the care of the ultimate end, and be directed by his rule.[16]

[111] Because the priesthood of the gentiles and the whole worship of their gods existed merely for the acquisition of temporal goods (which were all ordained to the common good of the multitude, whose care devolved upon the king), the priests of the gentiles were very properly subject to the kings. Similarly, since in the old law earthly goods were promised to the religious people[17] (not indeed by demons[18] but by the true God), the priests of the old law, we read,[19] were also subject to the kings. But in the new law there is a higher priesthood by which men are guided

[14]*Populus Christianus*, i.e., the institutional unity of all Christians, whose head is the Pope "holding the apex of both powers, spiritual and temporal": 2 *Sent.*, 44, *exp. text.* (*VIII, p. 106). All-important in Aquinas' political thought, this notion was for the first time criticized by the Dominican JOHN OF PARIS, A.D. 1302; see CG 4, 76 (*VII, p. 105) and JOHN OF PARIS' corrections of this text (Appendix II, *loc. cit.*)

[15]Ps.-CYRIL OF ALEXANDRIA: [*Romano Pontifici*] *primates mundi tamquam ipsi Domino Iesu Christo obediunt.* The text is quoted in C. *Impugn.* 3 (IV, 29); 4 *Sent.*, 24, III, 2 sol. 2; C. *Errores Graecorum* 2 (III, 324). The *Liber Thesaurorum* from which this authority was drawn is a compilation of texts of the Greek Fathers, made by Aquinas' contemporary and confrère BONACURSIUS (*Script. O. P.* I, 156, 159). In regard to the doctrine cf. 2 *Sent.*, 44, *exp. text.* (*VIII, p. 106); 4 *Sent.*, 37, *exp. text.; CG* IV, 76 (*VII, p. 105); *Summa* II-II, 60, 6 ad 3. Best interpretation of this passage *apud* GILSON, *Dante* 183 f, 206 ff; *Id., La philosophie au MA* 570 ff.

[16]See above note 8.

[17]"As is clear from *Levit.* xxvi and *Deut.* xxviii", *In Ep. Ad Rom.* IX, 1: *Summa* I-II, 114, 10 *in* 1.

[18]This was taught by the Manicheans and the Waldenses.

[19]See the quotations from Holy Scripture in GREGORY IX, *Decretales* I, 33. 6 (c. *Solitae Benignitatis*), FRIEDBERG 197.

to heavenly goods. Consequently, in the law of Christ, kings must be subject to priests.

[112] It was therefore also a marvellous disposition of Divine Providence that, in the city of Rome, which God had foreseen would be the principal seat of the Christian priesthood, the custom was gradually established that the rulers of the city should be subject to the priests, for as VALERIUS MAXIMUS[20] relates: "Our city has always considered that everything should yield precedence to religion, even those things in which it aimed to display the splendour of supreme majesty. We therefore unhesitatingly made the imperial dignity minister to religion, considering that the empire would thus hold control of human affairs if faithfully and constantly it were submissive to the divine power."

[113] And because it was to come to pass that the religion of the Christian priesthood should especially thrive in France, God provided that among the Gauls too their tribal priests, called Druids, should lay down the law of all Gaul, as JULIUS CAESAR[21] relates in the book which he wrote about the Gallic war.

CHAPTER IV (I, 15)

THAT REGAL GOVERNMENT SHOULD BE ORDAINED PRINCIPALLY TO ETERNAL BEATITUDE

[114] As the life by which men live well here on earth is ordained, as to its end, to that blessed life which we hope for in heaven, so too whatever particular goods are procured by man's agency—whether wealth, profits, health, eloquence, or learning—are

[20] I, 1, 9.
[21] De Bello Gallico VI, 13, 5.

ordained to the good life of the multitude. If, then, as we have said, the person who is charged with the care of our ultimate end ought to be over those who have charge of things ordained to that end, and to direct them by his rule, it clearly follows that, just as the king ought to be subject to the divine government administered by the office of priesthood, so he ought to preside over all human offices, and regulate them by the rule of his government.

[115] Now anyone on whom it devolves to do something which is ordained to another thing as to its end is bound to see that his work is suitable to that end; thus, for example, the armourer so fashions the sword that it is suitable for fighting, and the builder should so lay out the house that it is suitable for habitation. Therefore, since the beatitude of heaven is the end of that virtuous life which we live at present, it pertains to the king's office to promote the good life of the multitude in such a way as to make it suitable for the attainment of heavenly happiness, that is to say, he should command those things which lead to the happiness of Heaven and, as far as possible,[1] forbid the contrary.

[116] What conduces to true beatitude and what hinders it are learned from the law of God, the teaching of which belongs to the office of the priest, according to the words of Malachy:[2] "The lips of the priest shall guard knowledge and they shall seek the law from his mouth." Wherefore the Lord prescribes in the Book of Deuteronomy[3] that "after he is raised to the throne of his kingdom, the king shall copy out to himself the Deutoronomy of this law, in a volume,

---

[1] Summa I-II, 96, 2.   [2] ii, 7.   [3] xvii, 18-19.

taking the copy of the priests of the Levitical tribe, he shall have it with him and shall read it all the days of his life, that he may learn to fear the Lord his God, and keep his words and ceremonies which are commanded in the law." Thus the king, taught the law of God, should have for his principal concern the means by which the multitude subject to him may live well.

[117] This concern is threefold: first of all, to establish a virtuous life in the multitude subject to him; second, to preserve it once established; and third, having preserved it, to promote its greater perfection.

[118] For an individual man to lead a good life two things are required. The first and most important is to act in a virtuous manner (for virtue is that by which one lives well[4]); the second, which is secondary and instrumental,[5] is a sufficiency of those bodily goods whose use is necessary for virtuous life. Yet the unity of man is brought about by nature, while the unity of multitude, which we call peace, must be procured through the efforts of the ruler. Therefore, to establish virtuous living in a multitude three things are necessary. First of all, that the multitude be established in the unity of peace. Second, that the multitude thus united in the bond of peace, be directed to acting well. For just as a man can do nothing well unless unity within his members be presupposed, so a multitude of men lacking the unity of peace will be hindered from virtuous action by the fact that it is fighting against itself. In the third place, it is necessary that there be at hand a sufficient supply of the things required for proper living, procured by the ruler's efforts.

---

[4] ST. AUGUSTINE, De Libero Arbitrio II, 19: PL 32, 1268.
[5] ARISTOTLE, Eth. Nic. I, 8: 1099b 1, 28. In Eth. I, 14: 173.

[119] When virtuous living is set up in the multitude by the efforts of the king, it then remains for him to look to its conservation. Now there are three things which prevent the permanence of the public good. One of these arises from nature. The good of the multitude should not be established for one time only; it should be in a sense perpetual. Men, on the other hand, cannot abide forever, because they are mortal. Even while they are alive they do not always preserve the same vigour, for the life of man is subject to many changes, and thus a man is not equally suited to the performance of the same duties throughout the whole span of his life. A second impediment to the preservation of the public good, which comes from within, consists in the perversity of the wills of men, inasmuch as they are either too lazy to perform what the commonweal demands, or, still further, they are harmful to the peace of the multitude because, by transgressing justice, they disturb the peace of others. The third hindrance to the preservation of the commonweal comes from without, namely, when peace is destroyed through the attacks of enemies and, as it sometimes happens, the kingdom or city is completely blotted out.

[120] In regard to these three dangers, a triple charge is laid upon the king. First of all, he must take care of the appointment of men to succeed or replace others in charge of the various offices. Just as in regard to corruptible things (which cannot remain the same forever) the government of God made provision that through generation one would take the place of another in order that, in this way, the integrity of the

universe might be maintained,[6] so too the good of the multitude subject to the king will be preserved through his care when he sets himself to attend to the appointment of new men to fill the place of those who drop out. In the second place, by his laws and orders, punishments and rewards, he should restrain the men subject to him from wickedness and induce them to virtuous deeds, following the example of God, Who gave His law to man and requites those who observe it with rewards, and those who transgress it with punishments. The king's third charge is to keep the multitude entrusted to him safe from the enemy, for it would be useless to prevent internal dangers if the multitude could not be defended against external dangers.

[121] Finally, for the proper direction of the multitude there remains the third duty of the kingly office, namely, that he be solicitous for its improvement. He performs this duty when, in each of the things we have mentioned, he corrects what is out of order and supplies what is lacking, and if any of them can be done better he tries to do so. This is why the Apostle[7] exhorts the faithful to be "zealous for the better gifts."

[122] These then are the duties of the kingly office, each of which must now be treated in greater detail.

[6] Cf. CG IV, 97; De Potentia V, 5.
[7] I Cor. xii, 31.

CHAPTER V (II, 1)

That It Belongs to the Office of a King to Found the City

[123] We must begin[1] by explaining the duties of a king with regard to the founding of a city or kingdom. For, as Vegetius[2] declares, "the mightiest nations and most commended kings thought it their greatest glory either to found new cities or have their names made part of, and in some way added to, the names of cities already founded by others." This, indeed, is in accord with Holy Scripture, for the Wise Man says in *Ecclesiasticus*:[3] "The building of a city shall establish a name." The name of Romulus, for instance, would be unknown today had he not founded the city of Rome.

[124] Now in founding a city or kingdom, the first step is the choice, if any be given, of its location.[4] A temperate region should be chosen, for the inhabitants derive many advantages from a temperate climate. In the first place, it ensures them health of body and length of life; for, since good health consists in the right temperature of the vital fluids,[5] it follows that

[1] See above § 100, p. 57.   [2] *De Re Militari* IV, *prol.*   [3] xl, 19.

[4] See Introduction p. xxxiii f. In *Pol.* VII, 1; 1357b 19, Aristotle states a similar problem: what sort of natural endowment the members of the ideal city ought to have.

[5] Aristotle, *Physics* VII, 3: 246b 4. *In Phys.* VII, 5, 3; *Summa* I-II, 49, 2 *ad* 1. "Long before Aristotle, probably before Hippocrates, it was held that, corresponding to the four elements, fire, air, water, earth, and the four qualities, hot, cold, moist, dry, are the four humors of the body, viz., blood, phlegm, yellow bile, and black bile. These three sets of elements, qualities and humors could then be brought, by permutation and combination, into a complex system of arrangements, based upon the following scheme: hot + moist = blood; hot + dry = yellow bile; cold + moist = phlegm; cold + dry = black bile, the different combinations giving the qualitative aspects of disease, and, by the same token, of the physiologic action of drugs. The whole arrangement made up the 'humoral pathology' which regarded health

health will be best preserved in a temperate clime,[6] because like is preserved by like. Should, however, heat or cold be excessive, it needs must be that the condition of the body will be affected by the condition of the atmosphere; whence some animals instinctively migrate in cold weather to warmer regions, and in warm weather return to the colder places,[7] in order to obtain, through the contrary dispositions of both locality and weather, the due temperature of their humours.

[125] Again, since it is warmth and moisture that preserve animal life,[8] if the heat is intense the natural moisture[9] of the body is dried up and life fails, just as a lantern is extinguished if the liquid poured into it be quickly consumed by too great a flame. Whence it is said that in certain very torrid parts of Ethiopia a man cannot live longer than thirty years.[10] On the other hand, in extremely cold regions the natural moisture is easily frozen and the natural heat soon lost.

[126] Then, too, a temperate climate is most conducive to fitness for war, by which human society is

---

and disease as the proper adjustment or imbalance respectively of the different components mentioned, and the scheme was further elaborated by GALEN and the Arabian physicians, in that remedies and their compounds were classified in numerical scales according to the 'degree' or relative proportions of their several qualities." GARRISON 77.

[6] ARISTOTLE, De Longitudine et Brevitate Vitae 1: 465a 7. Cf. ST. ALBERT, De Morte et Vita II, 1: Opera IX, 351; Id., De Natura Locorum II, 2 ff: ibid. 560 ff.

[7] Cf. ARISTOTLE, Hist. Anim. VIII, 12: 596b 20 ff.

[8] ARISTOTLE, De Longit. et Brev. Vitae 5: 466a 20: "An animal is by nature humid and warm, and to live is to be of such a constitution, while old age is dry and cold . . . The material constituting the bodies of all things consists of . . . the hot and the cold, the dry and the moist." On mediaeval expressions of this theory see ALFRED OF SARESHEL, De Motu Cordis XIII, 3; 64; ST. ALBERT, De Morte et Vita II, 4; IX, 357.

[9] In Latin naturale humidum. On some theological applications of this notion in St. Thomas' teaching see 4 Sent., 49, I, 2, 3; Summa I, 119, 1.

[10] ST. ALBERT relates the same fact in De Natura Locorum II, 3: IX, 563.

kept in security. As VEGETIUS[11] tells us, "all peoples
that live near the sun and are dried up by the excessive heat have keener wits but less blood, so that they
possess no constancy or self-reliance in hand-to-hand
fighting; for, knowing they have but little blood, they
have great fear of wounds. On the other hand, Northern
tribes, far removed from the burning rays of the sun,
are more dull-witted indeed, but because they have
an ample flow of blood, they are ever ready for war.
Those who dwell in temperate climes have, on the
one hand, an abundance of blood and thus make light
of wounds or death, and, on the other hand, no lack
of prudence, which puts a proper restraint on them in
camp and is of great advantage in war and peace as
well."

[127] Finally, a temperate climate is of no little
value for political life. As ARISTOTLE says in his *Politics*:[12] "Peoples that dwell in cold countries[13] are full
of spirit but have little intelligence and little skill.
Consequently they maintain their liberty better but
have no political life and (through lack of prudence)
show no capacity for governing others. Those who
live in hot regions[14] are keen-witted and skilful in the
things of the mind but possess little spirit, and so are
in continuous subjection and servitude. But those who
live between these extremes of climate[15] are both
spirited and intelligent; hence they are continuously

[11] *De Re Militari* I, 2; this chapter deals with the question from what
regions military recruits are to be conscripted.
[12] VII, 7: 1327b 23-32. The view that the character of different peoples
varies with the different climatic conditions is common among all
classical geographers.   On mediaeval re-affirmations of this view see
KIMBLE 176 ff.
[13] ARISTOTLE adds: particularly the peoples of Europe.
[14] *i.e.*, "the peoples of Asia".
[15] *i.e.*, "the Greek stock . . . if only it could once achieve political
unity."

free, their political life is very much developed, and
they are capable of ruling others." Therefore, a temperate region should be chosen for the foundation of
a city or a kingdom.

CHAPTER VI (II, 2)

THAT THE CITY SHOULD HAVE WHOLESOME AIR

[128] After deciding on the locality of the kingdom,
the king must select a site suitable for building a city.
[129] Now the first requisite would seem to be wholesome air, for civil life presupposes natural life, whose
health in turn depends on the wholesomeness of the
air. According to VITRUVIUS,[1] the most healthful spot
is "a high place, troubled neither by mists nor frosts
and facing neither the sultry nor the chilly parts of
the sky. Also, it should not lie near marsh country."
The altitude of the place contributes to the wholesomeness of the atmosphere because highlands are open to
all the breezes which purify the air; besides, the
vapours, which the strength of the sun's rays causes
to rise from the earth and waters, are more dense in
valleys and in low-lying places than in highlands,
whence it is that the air on mountains is rarer. Now
this rarified air, which is the best for easy and natural
breathing, is vitiated by mists and frosts which are
frequent in very damp places; as a consequence, such
places are found to be inimical to health. Since marshy
districts have an excess of humidity, the place chosen
for the building of a city must be far from any

---

[1] De Architectura I, 4. In §§ 129 and 130 the quotation marks indicate
that the passages are taken, more or less literally, from Vitruvius'
work, l.c.

marshes. "For when the morning breezes come at sunrise to such a place, and the mists that rise from the swamps join them, they will scatter through the town the breath of the poisonous beasts of the marshes mingled with the mist, and will render the site pestilential." "Should, however, the walls be built in marshes that lie along the coast and face the north (or thereabouts[2]) and if these marshes be higher than the seashore, they would seem to be quite reasonably built, since, by digging ditches, a way will be opened to drain the water of the marshes into the sea, and when storms swell the sea it will flow back into the marshes and thus prevent the propagation of the animals there. And if any animals come down from higher places, the unwonted saltiness of the water will destroy them."

[130] Further provision for the proper proportion of heat and cold must be made when laying out the city by having it face the correct part of the sky. "If the walls, particularly of a town built on the coast, face the south, it will not be healthy," since such a locality will be cold in the morning, for the rays of the sun do not reach it, but at noon will be baked in the full glare of the sun. As to places that face the west, at sunrise they are cool or even cold, at noon quite warm, and in the evening unpleasantly hot, both on account of the long-continued heat and the exposure to the sun. On the other hand, if it has an eastern exposure, in the morning, with the sun directly opposite, it will be moderately warm, at noon it will not be much warmer since the sun does not reach it directly, but in the evening it will be cold as the rays

[2]VITRUVIUS says: . . . or between the north and east.

of the sun will be entirely on the other side. And there
will be the same or a similar proportion of heat and
cold if the town faces the north. By experience we
may learn that the change from cold to heat is un-
healthy. "Animals which are transferred from cold
to warm regions cannot endure but are dissolved,"
"since the heat sucks up their moisture and weakens
their natural strength;" whence even in salubrious
districts "all bodies become weak from the heat."³

[131] Again, since suitable food is very helpful for
preserving health, we must further judge of the salu-
brity of a place which has been chosen as a town-site
by the condition of the food which grows upon its
soil. The ancients⁴ were wont to explore this condition by examining the animals raised on the spot. For
man, like other animals, finds nourishment in the
products of the earth. Hence, if in a given place we
kill some animals and find their entrails⁵ to be sound,
the conclusion will be justified that man also will get
good food in the same place. If, however, the members

³ In Latin *redduntur*. At this point a certain small number of MSS
put the end of St. Thomas' authentic treatise, while the larger part
of the MSS has the end at the word *recreentur*, below § 148, p. 80. ALFRED
O'RAHILLY (*Irish Eccles. Rec.* XXXI, 406) gives the following explanation of these facts. "The words which immediately follow *redduntur*
are these: *Quia vero ad corporum sanitatem* [§ 131]. Now, after *recreentur* [§ 148] [certain MSS] add *Quia vero etctera* or *Quia vero*,
i.e. the first words of the section which follows *redduntur*. This is for-
tunately made quite clear by the MS Brussels, *Bibl. Royale* 1573, in
which the scribe wrote the words *Quia vero etcetera, ut supra de
ciborum salubritate etc.*, and then crossed them out. It seems clear,
then, that in the original from which some of the MSS were copied
there was, immediately following *recreentur* [§ 148], a section beginning *Quia vero ad corporum sanitatem* [§ 131] . . . down to *recreentur*
again, thus duplicating the passage. This extra bit, having become
detached from another copy, *and thus leaving it to end at redduntur*,
got tacked on to the end of an already complete copy, thus providing
a duplication — *ut supra*, as above — of the passage which began
Quia vero etc. The problem [of this shorter ending] is therefore neatly
solved." See Introduction, note 91, p. xxvi.
⁴ VITRUVIUS, *loc. cit.*
. . ⁵ *Ibid.* VITRUVIUS speaks of the condition of their livers.

of these animals should be found diseased, we may reasonably infer that that country is no healthy place for men either.

[132] Just as a temperate climate must be sought, so good water must be made the object of investigation. For the body depends for its health on those things which men more frequently put to their use. With regard to the air it is clear that, breathing it continuously, we draw it down into our very vitals; as a result, purity of air is what conduces most to the preservation of men. But of all things put to use as nourishment, water is used most frequently both as drink and food. Nothing therefore, except good air, so much helps to make a district healthy as does pure water.

[133] There is still another means of judging the healthfulness of a place, i.e., by the ruddy complexion of the inhabitants, their sturdy, well-shaped limbs, the presence of many and vivacious children, and of many old people. On the other hand, there can be no doubt about the deadliness of a climate where people are misshapen and weak, their limbs either withering or swollen beyond proportion, where children are few and sickly, and old people rather scarce.

CHAPTER VII (II, 3)

THAT THE CITY SHOULD HAVE AN ABUNDANT SUPPLY OF FOOD

[134] It is not enough, however, that the place chosen for the site of a city be such as to preserve the health of the inhabitants; it must also be sufficiently

fertile to provide food.[1] A multitude of men cannot
live where there is not a sufficient supply of food.
Thus VITRUVIUS[2] narrates that when Dinocrates,[3] a
brilliant architect, was explaining to Alexander of
Macedon that a beautifully laid out city could be built
upon a certain mountain,[4] Alexander asked whether
there were fields that could supply the city with sufficient grain. Finding out that there were not, he said
that an architect who would build a city on such a site
would be blameworthy. For "just as a newborn infant
cannot be fed nor made to grow as it should, except
on the nurse's milk, so a city cannot have a large
population without a large supply of foodstuffs."

[135] Now there are two ways in which an abundance of foodstuffs can be supplied to a city. The first
we have already mentioned, where the soil is so fertile
that it amply provides for all the necessities of human
life. The second is by trade, through which the necessaries of life are brought to the town in sufficient
quantity from different places.

[136] It is quite clear that the first means is better.
The more dignified a thing is, the more self-sufficient
it is, since whatever needs another's help is by that
fact proven to be deficient.[5] Now the city which is
supplied by the surrounding country with all its vital
needs is more self-sufficient than another which must
obtain those supplies by trade. A city therefore which

---

[1] Cf. VITRUVIUS I, 5.   [2] Op. cit. II prol.
[3] DINOCRATES was a Macedonian architect employed by ALEXANDER in
the building of Alexandria in Egypt; Pauly-Wissowa V. 2392.
[4] The Mount Athos. I have shaped this mountain, says DINOCRATES
according to VITRUVIUS, into the figure of the statue of a man, in whose
left hand I have shown the ramparts of a very extensive city; in his
right a bowl to receive the waters of all the rivers which are in that
mountain.
[5] Cf. ARISTOTLE, Eth. Nic. I, 5: 1097b 7-11. In Eth. I, 9: 114; ibid. VIII,
6: 1615, et alibi; Summa II-II, 188, 8.

has an abundance of food from its own territory is more dignified than one which is provisioned through trade.

[137] It seems that self-sufficiency is also safer, for the import of supplies and the access of merchants can easily be prevented whether owing to wars or to the many hazards of the sea,[6] and thus the city may be overcome through lack of food.

[138] Moreover, this first method of supply is more conducive to the preservation of civic life. A city which must engage in much trade in order to supply its needs also has to put up with the continuous presence of foreigners. But intercourse with foreigners, according to ARISTOTLE's Politics,[7] is particularly harmful to civic customs. For it is inevitable that strangers, brought up under other laws and customs, will in many cases act as the citizens are not wont to act and thus, since the citizens are drawn by their example to act likewise, their own civic life is upset.

[139] Again, if the citizens themselves devote their life to matters of trade, the way will be opened to many vices. Since the foremost tendency of tradesmen is to make money,[8] greed is awakened in the hearts of the citizens through the pursuit of trade. The result is that everything in the city will become venal; good faith will be destroyed and the way opened to all kinds of trickery; each one will work only for his own profit, despising the public good; the cultivation of virtue will fail since honour, virtue's reward, will be

---

[6] In Latin maris discrimina (See Appendix I, p. 90).
[7] V, 3: 1303a 27; also VII, 6: 1327a 13-15.
[8] ARISTOTLE, Pol. I, 9: 1257b 22; Eth. Nic. I, 3: 1096a 3. In Pol. I, 7 and 8; In Eth. I, 5: 70-72; Summa I-II, 2, 1; II-II, 77, 4. On the Greek evaluation of trade and tradesmen see NEWMAN I, 99 ff, esp. 103, 105, 129; on the Patristic and mediaeval attitude O'BRIEN 136 ff; PIRENNE 109 ff.

bestowed upon the rich. Thus, in such a city, civic life will necessarily be corrupted. [140] The pursuit of trade is also very unfavourable to military activity.[9] Tradesmen, not being used to the open air and not doing any hard work but enjoying all pleasures, grow soft in spirit and their bodies are weakened and rendered unsuited to military labours. In accordance with this view, Civil Law[10] forbids soldiers to engage in business.

[141] Finally, that city enjoys a greater measure of peace whose people are more sparsely assembled together and dwell in smaller proportion within the walls of the town, for when men are crowded together it is an occasion for quarrels and all the elements for seditious plots are provided. Hence, according to ARISTOTLE's doctrine,[11] it is more profitable to have the people engaged outside the cities than for them to dwell constantly within the walls. But if a city is dependent on trade, it is of prime importance that the citizens stay within the town and there engage in trade. It is better, therefore, that the supplies of food be furnished to the city from its own fields than that it be wholly dependent on trade.

[9] Cf. VEGETIUS, *De Re Militari* I, 3: "I believe that there is no question but that rustic people are better for military service, bred as they are in the open air and on hard work. For they are inured to the sun, they do not seek the shade, are ignorant of pleasures and refinements, simple of mind, content with little. Their limbs have been hardened to every toil and they are used to carrying coats of mail, to digging ditches and heaving loads." St. Thomas adapts this text to the problem of merchants.

[10] Codex IUSTINIANI I, 12, 34: *Negotiatores ne militent.*

[11] *Pol.* VI, 4: 1318b 9-15. WILLIAM OF MOERBEKA translated this passage thus: *optimus enim populus, qui terrae cultivus est . . . ubi vivit multitudo ab agricultura vel pascuis . . . Non vacans, ut non saepe congregationes faciat. Propterea . . . aliena non concupiscunt, sed delectabilius est ipsis laborare quam politizare et principari* (SUSEMIHL 466 f.) St. Thomas misunderstood the words *congregationes facere* which he took to mean "the crowding and dwelling of the people within the walls of the town," while ARISTOTLE speaks of civic assemblies.

[142] Still, trade must not be entirely kept out of a city, since one cannot easily find any place so overflowing with the necessaries of life as not to need some commodities from other parts. Also, when there is an over-abundance of some commodities in one place, these goods would serve no purpose if they could not be carried elsewhere by professional traders. Consequently, the perfect city will make a moderate use of merchants.

CHAPTER VIII (II, 4)

THAT THE CITY SHOULD HAVE A PLEASANT SITE

[143] A further requisite when choosing a site for the founding of a city is this, that it must charm the inhabitants by its beauty. A spot where life is pleasant will not easily be abandoned nor will men commonly be ready to flock to unpleasant places, since the life of man cannot endure without enjoyment. It belongs to the beauty of a place that it have a broad expanse of meadows, an abundant forest growth, mountains to be seen close at hand, pleasant groves and a copiousness of water.

[144] However, if a country is too beautiful, it will draw men to indulge in pleasures,[1] and this is most harmful to a city. In the first place, when men give themselves up to pleasure their senses are dulled, since this sweetness immerses the soul in the senses so that man cannot pass free judgment on the things

[1]See Introduction p. xxv.

which cause delight. Whence, according to ARISTOTLE'S sentence, the judgment of prudence is corrupted by pleasure.[2]

[145] Again, indulgence in superfluous pleasure leads from the path of virtue, for nothing conduces more easily to immoderate increase which upsets the mean of virtue, than pleasure. Pleasure is, by its very nature, greedy, and thus on a slight occasion one is precipitated into the seductions of shameful pleasures just as a little spark is sufficient to kindle dry wood: moreover, indulgence does not satisfy the appetite for the first sip only makes the thirst all the keener. Consequently, it is part of virtue's task to lead men to refrain from pleasures. By thus avoiding any excess, the mean of virtue will be more easily attained.

[146] Also, they who give themselves up to pleasures grow soft in spirit and become weak-minded when it is a question of tackling some difficult enterprise, enduring toil, and facing dangers. Whence, too, indulgence in pleasures is detrimental to warfare, as VEGETIUS puts it in his *On the Art of Knighthood*:[3] "He fears death less who knows that he has had little pleasure in life."

[147] Finally, men who have become dissolute through pleasures usually grow lazy and, neglecting necessary matters and all the pursuits that duty lays upon them, devote themselves wholly to the quest of pleasure, on which they squander all that others had so carefully amassed. Thus, reduced to poverty and yet unable to deprive themselves of their wonted pleasures, they do not shrink from stealing and robbing

---

[2] ARISTOTLE, *Eth. Nic.* VI, 5: 1140b 11-21. *In Eth.* VI, 4: 1169 f.
[3] *De Re Militari* I, 3.

in order to have the wherewithal to indulge their craving for pleasure.

[148] It is therefore harmful to a city to superabound in delightful things, whether it be on account of its situation or from whatever other cause. However, in human intercourse it is best to have a moderate share of pleasure as a spice of life, so to speak, wherein man's mind may find some recreation.[4]

⁴ In Latin *ut animi hominum recreentur*. See above § 130, note 3, p. 73.

APPENDIX I

SELECTED VARIANTS

Sigla Codicum

A—Bologna, Biblioteca universitaria, Cod. 861 (1655), fol. 33ra-38vb. *Expl.* recreentur. Quia vero etc. supra.

B—Paris, Bibliothèque de Sainte-Geneviève, Cod. 238, fol. 160rb-166ra. *Expl.* recreentur.

C¹—Paris, Bibliothèque nationale, Lat. 14546 (Cod. Victorinus 635), fol. 163vb-175rb. *Expl.* diffusius documentum eidem tradidit. Hinc (*i.e. cap. II*, 5, circa medium, operis De Regimine Principum Tolomeo a Lucca attributi; vide A. O'Rahilly, Irish Ecclesiastical Record, vol. XXXI, p. 614.)

C²—*Idem codex cum correctionibus in margine et textu positis. Hic desinit fol.* 174ra, *ubi ad verba:* corpora aestate infirma redduntur (*De Regno II*, 6=II, 2) corrector animadvertit: abhinc incorreptus quia in alio plus non erat.

D—Codex Latinus Ottobonianus 198, fol. 191ra-197vb. *Expl.* recreentur.

E—Toledo, Biblioteca del Cabildo, Ms 19-15, fol. 78ra-86rb. *Expl.* recreentur.

F—Vatican., Cod. Lat. 773, fol. 87ra-93rb. *Expl.* infirma reducuntur. Explicit quod fecit.

G—Vatican., Cod. Lat. 807, fol. 192ra-210ra. *Expl.* recreentur.

p—Editio Piana: Divi Thomae Aquinatis Opuscula Omnia (t. XIII editionis Operum), Romae, 1570, fol. 160vb-168va.

Nota. Cum omnium quae vidimus manuscriptorum testimonium stat contra editionem vulgatam, siglum MSS adhibetur.

VARIAE LECTIONES TEXTUS

[4] ut sit animal sociale *ABDEFGp*   ut sit animal sociabile
C

[6] per rationem valente ex naturalibus principiis *MSS*
... ex universalibus principiis *p*

[7] alia animalia passiones alias diversis modis *CD(hom)*
FG(hom)   ... passiones aliquas diversis *B*   ... passiones
suas diversis *AEp*

[9] in (*om A*) omnibus quae in unum ordinantur, aliquid
invenitur alterius regitivum (regimen *A*) *ABDEFGp*   ...
quae ordinantur, aliquid invenitur altius *C*

[13] bonum commune multitudinis et non suum (proprium
A) quaerens *MSS*   ... suum commodum quaerens *p*

[14] in uno autem vico *ABDEFG*   ... viro *C*   ...
dico *p*

[18] uniri autem dicuntur *ABDEFGp*   unum autem
dicuntur *C* ‖ eo quod appropinquant ad unum *BDFGp*
eo quod appropinquat ad unum *ACE*

[19] quod movet principaliter *ABDEFG*   quod movet
primum *C* quod omnia movet *p*

[23] magis igitur (enim *E* autem *A*) est noxia (nociva *p*)
tyrannis quam oligarchia, oligarchia autem quam democratia
ABDEFGp   magis igitur est noxia tyrannis quam oligarchia
et quam democratia *C*

[25] bonum provenit in rebus ex una causa perfecta
ABC'DEFGp   ... ex una causa tantum perfecta *C²*

[26] nec firmari quidquam potest quale sit quod positum
MSS   ... potest quod positum *p*

[27] dominationem non ferant. Conantur etiam ne inter
MSS   ... ferant ne inter *p*

[28] iuxta sententiam Aristotelis *MSS*   ... sententiam
Philosophi *p*

[30] Quia igitur optimum et pessimum regnum existit *BDF*
... pessimum regimen existit *EG*   ... pessimum existit
C   ... pessimum consistunt *p*

[35] sive dum hoc desideratur *MSS*   sive dum hoc con-
sideratur *p*

[37] bono pacis quod est praecipuum in multitudine sociali

APPENDIX I

85

C^2DEGp bono pacis praecipuum *B* . . . quod est principium in C^1F

[38] non statim sequitur ut totaliter ad subditorum *MSS*
. . . sequitur ut ad subditorum *p*

[39] ex his quae pro tempore fuerunt *Ep* ex his quae (*om* C^1) per (*om F*) tempora fiunt *CF* ex his quae (*om BDG*) pro tempore fiunt *ABDG* || ut in Romana republica maxime apparet *MSS* . . . . manifeste apparet *p*

[42] Quaesivit sibi Dominus virum secundum cor suum et praecepit ei Dominus ut esset dux super populum suum. Deinde *MSS* . . . cor suum. Deinde *p*

[46] docet nos Petrus non solum bonis *ABDEFGp* docet nos potius non solum bonis *C*

[49] rex institutus potest destitui *ABCDEG* . . . potest destrui *Fp* || si potestate regia ut (*om DG*) tyrannide abutatur *CDG* . . . regia tyrannice abutatur *ABEFp* || pactum a subditis non servetur *ABDEFG* . . . . subditis non (*om* C^1) observetur *C* . . . subditis non reservetur *p* || Vespasiano patri . . . dum tyrannidem exerceret, omnibus (omnia *corr D*) quae idem perverse fecerat . . . revocatis (revocata *corr D*). Quo factum est ut *ABDEGp* . . . revocatis; quod factum est, et *CF*

[51] ut cor tyranni crudele convertat *ABEFGp* . . . crudele convertatur *CD(corr)* || Nabuchodonosor crudelem regem in tantam devotionem convertit BDC^2EFG . . . regem convertit AC^1p || Pharaonem tyrannidem exercentem in populo Dei deiecit cum exercitu eius in mare. Ipse *G* . . . exercitu eius. Ipse *D* Pharaonis (Pharaonem *B*) tyrannidem deiecit cum exercitu eius (suo *F*) in mare. Ipse *BCF* Pharaonem tyrannum cum exercitu suo deiecit in mare *E* Pharaonem tyrannum deiecit cum exercitu suo in mare *p* || requiem se daturum a labore et concussione et servitute *ABDEFG* a labore et confusione et servitute *Cp*

[55] ex opinionibus hominum et verbis eorum, quibus *ABCEF* . . . hominum, quibus *DGp*

[56] placere omnibus studet *BCDFG* placere hominibus studet *AEp* || pro qua magnanimis viris omnis debet esse contentio AC^1EFp . . . viris communis debet . . . *BDG* . . . viris omnibus debet . . . C^2

[57] sequitur quoddam mirabile ut quia virtuosos (virtuosus *DF*) actus consequitur (sequitur *AB*) gloria (om *FG*) ipsaque (itaque *DG*) gloria virtuose contemnitur, ex contemptu gloriae homo gloriosus (virtuosus *AF*) reddatur (redditur *DEG*) *MSS*   fit quoddam mirabile ut quia virtuosos actus sequitur gloria, ipsa gloria virtuose contemnatur et ex contemptu gloriae homo gloriosus reddatur *p* ‖ si igitur hoc solum praemium statuatur principibus *ACEF*   . . . hoc bonum praemium . . . *DG*   . . . hoc praemium . . . *B*   . . . hoc solum bonum statuatur praemium principibus *p*

[58] libertate patriae sub hostium servitute redacta *MSS* . . . sub hostibili potestate redacta *p*

[59] ambitio multos mortales falsos fieri *ABDEFGp* ambitio multos malos vel falsos fieri *C* ‖ hypocritos id est simulatores *ABDEFGp*   hypocritos et simulatores *C* ‖ periculosum est si sibi (ei *CF*) determinetur gloriae praemium *MSS*   periculosum est cum detinetur gloriae praemio *p*

[63] qui divitias habent amplius habere desiderant, qui voluptatibus fruuntur amplius perfrui desiderant et *ABCDG* . . . habere desiderant et *EFp*

[66] civis sanctorum et domesticus Dei *MSS*   civis et domesticus Dei *p*

[67] quod sublimem et eminentem *BC²EF*   quod eminentem *A*   quod et eminentem *C¹p* (*DG omittunt primam propositionem cap. IX*)

[69] in omnibus artibus et potentiis *ABDEFGp*   in omnibus actibus et potentiis *C*

[70] quam subdito pro recta actione *MSS*   . . . pro bona actione *p*

[72] dum hoc agit in regno quod Deus in mundo *ABDEFGp*   dum homo agit . . . *C* ‖ imperatores . . . divi vocabantur *BDEF*   . . . divini vocabantur *G*   . . . dii vocabantur *ACp*

[73] quid est sublimitas regis nisi *C²F*   quid est tempestas maris nisi *DGp*   quid est nisi *C¹* (*B habet lacunam, E scribit vocabulum sensu privatum*: tempel; *textus St. Gregorii: quid est potestas culminis nisi*) ‖ inter linguas sublimiter (et *add E*) honorantium et obsequia nimis humiliter salutantium non *AEF*   inter linguas nimis humiliter (*add C²*: orantium

et obsequia nimis humiliter) salutantium non C^1 inter
linguas honorantium (*lacuna*) et obsequia . . . *DG*   inter
linguas honorantium et extollentium non *B*   inter linguas
sublimantium et honorantium et obsequia . . . *p* || Deo suo
vero immolari *ABC^{a}DEGp*   Deo suo corde vero immolari
C^{a}F

[74] reges erunt et regnabunt cum *ABDEFGp*   reges
erunt cum *C*

[75] Econtra vero tyranni *MSS*   errant vero tyranni *p*

[78] amicitia super aliqua communione firmatur *ABDEFGp*
. . . communione fundatur *C* || eos enim qui conveniunt
ABDEFGp   omnes enim . . . *C* || nequaquam amant. Est
enim maioris virtutis inimicos diligere et persequentibus bene-
facere quam quod a multitudine observatur. Nec habent
tyranni *MSS*   nequaquam amant. Nec habent tyranni *p*

[81] ut fidelitatis (infidelitatis *F*) virtute *ABDEFGp*   ut
fidelitate virtutis *C* || timor autem est debile firmamentum
MSS   . . . debile fundamentum *p*

[83] Infelix autem rex qui populo *ABDEFGp*   . . . rex
cui populus *C*

[87] contra omnium communem libertatem laborat *ABFG*
contra omnem communem libertatem laborat *CE*   contra
omnem libertatem laborat *D*   contra omnium libertatem
laborat *p*

[89] quibus peccandi occasionem *MSS*   quibus apud Deum
peccandi occasionem *p*

[91] regibus abundanter temporalia bona (*om E*) proveniunt
MSS   regibus abundant temporalia bona et proveniunt *p*

[94] invenitur in homine non solum quantum ad hoc quod
ratio regit ceteras hominis partes, sed ulterius quantum
MSS   . . . ad hoc quod per rationem regitur unus homo, sed
etiam quantum *p*

[97] virtute animae formatur corpus *MSS*   virtute animae
informatur corpus *p*

[99] videlicet (scilicet *A*) diem a nocte *ABDEFGp*   dividit
diem a nocte *C*

[100] uniuscuiusque conditionem et statum *MSS*
uniuscuiusque constitutionem et statum *p*

[102] ex divina gubernatione sumenda est *MSS*   ex
gubernatione sumenda est *p*

[104] et quamvis nihil tale esse inveniatur in rebus praeter ipsum Deum *MSS*   . . . tale inveniatur in rebus post ipsum Deum *p* || multipliciter cura impenditur a diversis *CEF* multipliciter cura impeditur a diversis *ABDGp* || unde gubernatoris nomen assumitur *ABCDF*   unde gubernationis nomen assumitur *EG*   unde gubernationis ratio assumitur *p* || ut vita hominis conservetur; oeconomus *MSS*   . . . hominis conservetur in sanitate; oeconomus *p*

[105] est quoddam bonum extraneum homini *ABC'DEFGp*   . . . bonum extrinsecum homini *C²*

[106] si igitur finis ultimus hominis esset *MSS*   si igitur finis hominis esset *p* || animalia et servi (cervi *BG*) essent pars *ADEFp*   animalia etiam secundum hoc essent pars *C* || nunc autem videmus eos solos *BCDEFG*   sicut autem videmus . . . *A*   sicut videmus . . . *p*

[107] ut supra iam diximus, oportet autem eundem *MSS*   . . . oportet eundem *p*

[108] perducere ad illum (*om E*) ultimum finen *CDFG* perducere ad illum finem ultimum *A* (*B hom*)   perducere ad illum finem *p*

[112] Christiani sacerdotii principalem sedem *MSS* Christiani populi . . . *p*

[113] divinitus est provisum *MSS*   divinitus est permissum *p*

[114] ita ad bonam multitudinis vitam ordinantur *MSS* ita bonum multitudinis ordinatur *p* || sive divitae sive lucra *MSS*   sive divitiae suae lucra *p* || rex sicut divino regimini *MSS*   sicut dominio et regimini *p*

[116] cuius doctrina pertinet ad sacerdotum *ABC'DEFGp* cuius cognitio vel doctrina . . . *C²*

[119] dum transgrediendo iustitiam aliorum pacem disturbant *ABDEFGp*   dum transgrediendo iustitiam pacis aliorum . . . *C*

[120] ut vel sic conservetur integritas universi *BCDEGp* vel ut sic . . . *A*   ut universalis sic *F*

[121] ut sit de promotione sollicitus *ABEFGp*   ut sit de provisione sollicitus *C* (*D?*)

[123] primum igitur incipere oportet exponere *BCDEFG* primum igitur et praecipuum oportet exponere *A*   primum

igitur praecipue oportet exponere *p* ‖ principes commendati
nullam maiorem gloriam putaverunt *MSS*   principes nominati
nullam maiorem potuerunt gloriam assequi *p*

[124] primo quidem est regio eligenda *MSS*   . . . regio per
regem eligenda *p* ‖ ut ex contraria dispositione loci et temporis *BDF*   . . . loci temporis *CEp*

[127] ad politicam vitam non modicum valet *MSS*   ad
politicam vitam valet *p* ‖ quae autem in calidis locis sunt,
intellectivae quidem sunt et artificiosae secundum animan,
sine animositate autem (*om E*), propter quod (sibi *add B*)
subiectae quidem et servientes perseverant *BDEFG*   Qui
autem . . . artificiosae scientiae sed non animositate autem
propter quod . . . *C*   . . . propter quod subiectae (quidem
add p) sunt et subiectae perseverant *Ap* ‖ in mediis locis
habitant, et animositatem et intellectum habent; propter quod
ABC²DEFG   in mediis locis habitant propter quod *C^1* in
mediis locis habitant, utroque participant; propter quod *p*

[129] ut Vitruvius tradit *ADEG*   Victorinus *CF*
Victunus *B*   Vegetius *p* ‖ neque aestuosas neque frigidas
ABDEGp   neque aestuosus neque frigidus *CF* ‖ paludibus
non vicinus *ACDEFG*   . . . vicinis *B* . . . vicinas *p*

[130] si ad aquilonem locus urbis respiciat. Experimento
MSS   si ad aquilonem locus respiciat urbis, econverso est
quod de meridie respiciente est dictum. Experimento *p*

[131] quia vero ad corporum sanitatem convenientium (con-
veniens *A*) ciborum usus plurimum (*om AC*) confert (conferre
C), oportet salubritatem loci qui constituendae urbi eligitur
etiam (et *B*) ex conditione ciborum discernere qui nascuntur
in terra *ABCEG* (*D illegibilis propter conditionem repro-
ductionis photographicae*)   . . . ciborum usus requiritur, in
hoc conferre oportet de loci salubritate qui constituendae urbi
eligitur ut ex conditione ciborum discernatur qui nascuntur in
terra *p*

[132] manifestum est quod continue ipsum respirando
ABCEG (*D cf. supra*)   manifestum est quod quotidie ipsum
aspirando *p* ‖ ad incolumitatem hominum confert *MSS*
ad incolumitatem corporum confert *p* ‖ unde nihil praeter
(post *AB*) aeris puritatem magis pertinet ad loci sanitatem

quam aquarum salubritas *MSS*   ideo nihil est praeter aeris
puritatem magis pertinens ad . . . *p*

[133] exinanita membra vel inordinate tumentia *DEG*
. . . inordinate timentia *B*   . . . inordinatae mentis *AC*
exinanita membra vel morbida *p*

[134] unde Vitruvius: cum Dinocrates *E* (*nomen Vitruvii
discernitur in ABCDG, nomen vero Dinocratis in omnibus
praeter E corruptum est*)   unde, ut vult Philosophus, cum
Xenocrates *p* || interrogasse Alexandrum, si *BDEG*
interrogasse Alexander *A*   interrogasse Alexandrorum *C*
interrogasse fertur Alexander *p*

[136] quam si per mercationes abundet *ABDEG*   quam si
per mercatores abundet *Cp*

[137] diversa maris discrimina de facili potest impediri
deportatio victualium et accessus mercatorum ad locum; et
sic *E*   diversa viarum discrimina . . . *ACDG*   diversarum
via discrimina . . . *B*   diversa viarum discrimina de facili
potest impediri victualium deportatio et sic *p*

[138] ad conservationem civilem *BCDEG*   ad conver-
sationem civilem *Ap*

[139] quisque deserviet. Deficit virtutis studium, dum
honor virtutis deferetur divitibus *BDG*   . . . virtutis divitibus
deferetur *E*   . . . virtutis omnibus deferetur *AC*   quisque
deserviet deficietque virtutis studium, dum honor, virtutis
praemium, omnibus deferetur *p*

[140] est etiam (autem *G*) negotiationis usus nocivus quam
plurimum exercitio militari. Negotiatoribus namque, dum
umbram (membrum *B*) colunt, a laboribus vacant et fruuntur
deliciis, mollescunt animi (domini *E*) et corpora . . . *MSS*
est etiam negotiationis usus contrarius quam plurimum
exercitio militari. Negotiatores enim dum umbram colunt a
laboribus vacant, et dum fruuntur deliciis mollescunt animo
et corpora . . . *p*

[142] aliunde allatis. Eorum (eorumque *AE*) etiam (*om
ABC*) quae (quem *B om A*) in loco superabundant eodem
(eodemque *E*), reddetur inutilis copia, si *MSS*   aliunde
allatis eorumque quae in eodem loco superabundant, eodem
modo redderetur damnosa copia, si *p*

[143] non enim facile deseritur locus in quo delectabiliter
vivitur neque de facili *BDEG*   . . . locus vivitur neque de

facili *AC* . . . locus amoenus nec de facili *p* || ad loca illa
(locum illum *BCEG*) confluit (defluit *E*) hominum (habitantium *E*) multitudo quibus deest amoenitas, eo quod absque
delectatione hominum vita diu durare *MSS* ad locum
confluit habitantium multitudo cui deest amoenitas, eo quod
absque amoenitate vita hominis diu durare *p*
[144] verum nimia loci amoenitas superflue ad delicias
allicit homines, quod civitati plurimum nocet. Primo *MSS*
verum quia nimia amoenitas superflue ad . . . plurimum nocet,
ideo oportet ea moderate uti. Primo *p* || prudentiae iudicium
per delectationem corrumpitur *DEG* prudentiam iudicii . . .
A prudentia iudicii . . . *B* prudentia iudicis . . . *Cp*
[145] nihil autem facilius perducit *MSS* nihil autem magis
perducit *p* || et sic modica occasione sumpta *MSS* et sic
modica delectatione sumpta *p* || ut homines se a delecta-
tionibus abstrahant *BDG* . . . delectationibus extrahant *E*
. . . delectationibus abstineant *A* ut homines a delectationibus superfluis abstineant *p*
[146] ad pericula subeunda *MSS* ad pericula abhorrenda *p*

RUBRICAE IN MSS REPERTAE

*Nota. Rubricae codicis C hic negliguntur. Eaedem enim sunt
ac illae quae in editionibus vulgatis leguntur: quas antiquis
inscriptionibus deletis quidam amanuensis saeculi quintidecimi
huic codici inseruit.*

[2] (*rubrica*) Cap. I. Quid significetur nomine regis *BG* . . .
om. ADEF
[16] (*rubrica*) Cap. II. Quid plus expediat civitati (vel
provinciae *add F*) pluribus an uno regi rectore *BF* . . .
civitati vel obedire pluribus rectoribus aut uni regi *G* Quod
melius est unius regimen quam plurium *A* . . . *om DE*
[21] (*rubrica*) Cap. III. Quod regimen tyranni est pessimum
(regimen *add B*) *ABFG* *om DE*
[30] (*rubrica*) Cap. IV. Quare subditis regia dignitas redditur odiosa *BFG* . . . Quae pericula immineant a regis
dignitate *A* *om DE*
[36] (*rubrica*) Cap. V. Quod minus malum est (sequitur
G) cum (ex *B* si *G*) monarchia in tyrannidem convertitur

quam cum regnum (regimen *G*) plurium optimatum corrumpitur *BFG* . . . Quod pericula multa immineant ex multorum regimine *A* om *DE*

[41] (*rubrica*) Cap. VI. Qualiter providendum (praevidendum *G*) est ne rex incidat in tyrannidem *BG* ?*F* . . . De qualitate regentis et occursum (*sic*) contra tyrannum *A* om *DE*

[53] (*rubrica*) Cap. VII. Quod mundanus honor seu gloria non sunt sufficiens praemium regis *BG* . . . Quod solus honor non est praemium boni regis *A* De praemio regis capitulum primum *E* om *FD*

[61] (*rubrica*) Cap. VIII. Quod sufficiens praemium regis est a Deo expectandum *BG* . . . De vero praemio regis *A* De praemio regis capitulum secundum *E* om *FD*

[67] (*rubrica*) Cap. IX. Quem gradum in beatitudine tenuerint reges beati *BF* . . . Quem gradum obtinebunt in gloria reges *G* (*G sicut et D ex inadvertentia non distinxerunt cap. IX. Titulum huius capitis G praeposuit capiti sequenti*) . . . De excellentia praemii boni regis *A* Capitulum nonum. Quanta erit gloria regum bonorum *E* om *D*

[75] (*rubrica*) Cap. X. Quae bona perdunt tyranni quae regibus exhibentur (debentur *G*) *BFG* (de *G* vide supra) . . . Quae bona consequuntur bonum regentem *A* om *DE*

[86] (*rubrica*) Cap. XI. Quae supplicia sustinebunt tyranni *BFG* (de *G* vide supra) . . . De poena tyranni *A* om *DE*

[91] (*rubrica*) Cap XII. Recapitulatio huius primi libri *BF* (om *G*, vide supra) . . . Epilogus praedictorum *A* om *DE* qui tamen hoc caput distinguunt ope literae initialis.

[93] (*rubrica*) Incipit liber secundus. Cap. I. Quid sit regis officium *G* Incipit liber secundus de rege et regno (Cap. I add *B*) *BF* Cap. XIII. De regis officio in communi *A* om *DE* (*sed omnes praeter ACD initium libri secundi per literam initialem vel aliter significant*)

[96] (*rubrica*) Cap. II. Quid regi faciendum et quomodo *G* Cap. II. *reliqua* om *B* Cap. XIV. Quod institutio civitatis ad reges pertineat et qualiter *A* om *DEF*(?)

[102] (*rubrica*) Cap. III. Quod ratio gubernationis mundi (*sic*) ex divina gubernatione sumenda est *G* Cap. III. *reliqua* om *B* Cap. XV. De gubernatione regis *A* om *DEF*

[114] (*rubrica*) Cap. IV. Quod regnum ordinari debet ad beatitudinem sequendam principaliter *G*   Cap. IV *reliqua om B*   Cap. XVI. De his quae rex in regno suo debet intendere *A   om DE* ?*F*

[123] (*rubrica*) Cap. V. Quod ad officium regis spectat institutio civitatis *G*   Cap. V. *reliqua om B*   Cap. XVII. De electione regionis ad civitatem construendam *A   om DEF*

[128] (*rubrica*) Cap. VI. Quod civitas habeat aerem salubrem *G*   Cap. VI. *reliqua om B*   Cap XVIII. In quo (*sic*) civitas debet institui *A   om DE* ?*F*

[134] (*rubrica*) Cap. VII. Quod habeat libertatem propter motum (*lege*: . . . ubertatem propter victum) *G*   Cap. VII *reliqua om B*   Cap. XIX. De institutione civitatis in loci ubertate *A   om DE*

[143] (*rubrica*) Cap. VIII. Quod sit locus amoenus *G* Cap. VIII. *reliqua om B*   Cap. XX. De amoenitate loci instituendae civitatis *A   om DE*

APPENDIX II

SELECTED PARALLEL TEXTS

I. *Contra Impugnantes Dei Cultum et Religionem,* ch. 5 (ed. MANDONNET IV, 68.)

AVICENNA says: Nature did not give covering to man (as she gave hair to other animals), nor means of defence (as the oxen received horns and the lions claws); nor did nature prepare man's food (except the mother's milk). Instead of all this man was endowed with reason to provide for these things, and with hands to execute the providence of reason, as the Philosopher says.

AVICENNA[1] *De Anima (Sextus Naturalium)* V, 1: fol. 22rb: Man's actions possess certain properties which proceed from his soul and are not found in other animals. The first of these is that man's being in which he is created, could not last if he did not live in society. Man is not like other animals, each of which is self-sufficient for living with what it has by its nature. One man, on the contrary, if he were alone and left to rely on nothing but what he has by nature, would soon die, or at least his life would be miserable and certainly worse than it was meant to be. This is because of the nobility of man's nature and the ignobility of the nature of other beings. . . . It is necessary for man to add certain things to what nature gives him: he must needs prepare his food and also his clothing; for raw food, not treated by art, is unbecoming to him: he would not be able to live well with it. Likewise does he have to treat certain materials and make them into garments, while other animals have their covering by nature. First of all, then, man needs

---

[1] Arabian philosopher, died A.D. 1037.

the art of agriculture, and, in the second place, many
other arts. Now, one man would be unable to acquire
all these necessaries of life, if he were alone. . . . He
can do so, however, in society where one bakes the
other's bread and the latter in turn weaves the former's
clothes, and one man imports wares from far-away lands
for which he receives remuneration from the produce of
another man's country. These are the most evident
among many other reasons why it is necessary for man
to possess the natural ability to express to his fellow-
men what is in his mind. . . . The first and the easier
means of doing this is through the voice . . . [the other,
a more laborious one, being through gesture . . .] Nature
bestowed upon man's soul the faculty to compose out of
sounds a sign which is capable of being understood by
others. Other animals also utter sounds by which they
are able to indicate their wants. Yet these sounds have
but a natural and confused signification indicating only
in a general way what is wanted or not wanted. Human
sounds, on the contrary, may distinctly signify an infinite
range of wants. Hence they in their turn are infinite
in number.—Cf. PLATO, Republic II, 11 ff. (369B ff);
ARISTOTLE, Politics III, 9: 1280a 25 ff.

II. In Libros Ethicorum Aristotelis Expositio, Lib. I, lect. 1 (ed.
PIROTTA, n. 4).

. . . Man is by nature a social animal, since he stands in need
of many vital things which he cannot come by through his own
unaided effort (AVICENNA). Hence he is naturally part of a
group by which assistance is given him that he may live well.
He needs this assistance with a view to life as well as to the
good life. First, with a view to life, i.e., to having all those
things which are necessary for life and without which this
earthly life cannot be lived. In this regard, assistance is given
to man by the group called the household of which he is part.
For everyone has from his parents birth, nourishment and
education. Also all the members of the household or family
help one another in regard to the necessities of life. Assistance
of another kind comes to man by another group of which he

is part, assistance, that is, in view of the perfect fullness of life, in other words, that man may not only live but also live well, being equipped with all the things that make for the perfection of living. For this purpose, assistance comes to man from the civil group of which he is part. This assistance concerns not only man's corporal needs inasmuch as there are in a city many crafts which one household could not develop, but also his moral needs. Public power, indeed, by making itself feared, puts restraint upon those insolent youths who could not be corrected by paternal admonitions. [See *Summa* I-II, 95, 4.]

III. *In Libros Politicorum Aristotelis Expositio, Lib.* I, lect. 1.
[*Pol.* I, 2; 1252b 12: *The definition of the household.*[2]]
The Philosopher shows here for what purpose the community of the household is instituted. It is to be borne in mind that every human communication is built upon certain doings of men. There are some things which need to be done every day, such as eating, seeking protection from the cold, and such like. Other things do not have to be done daily, such as trading, fighting the enemy, and such like. Now it is natural for men to communicate and to help one another in both these kinds of work. Therefore, ARISTOTLE says, the household is a community naturally instituted for the life of every day, *i.e.,* for those works which have to be done daily.

[*Ibid.* 1252b 15: *The definition of the clan-village, called* vicus *in the mediaeval Latin translation.*]
Here the Philosopher speaks about the [next] community, *viz.,* the *vicus.* He calls *vicus* the first communication arising out of several households. It is the *first* communication after the household, since there is to follow another one, *viz.,* the city. The *vicus* is not instituted for the life of every day, as was the household, but with a view to needs not recurring daily. The members of this community do not come together to communicate concerning those things which are to be done daily, such as eating, and sitting by the fire, and such like, but

---

[2] The reader should compare these commentaries with the Aristotelian text so as to be able exactly to recognize the nature and extent of St. Thomas' exposition.

concerning external works transcending the daily round of necessities.

[*Ibid*. 1252b 16: *The vicus appears to be most natural.*]
The Philosopher says that the neighbourhood or vicinity of houses (which is the *vicus*) appears to be a most natural form of community; for nothing is more natural in the realm of live beings than the propagation of many from one: and this constitutes the *cluster of homes* (*vicinia domorum*.)

[*Ibid*. 1252b 27: *The definition of the city.*]
The Philosopher shows that in the nature of a city there are three essential characteristics. His first point is to determine what are the material elements of the city. Just as the *vicus* is composed of several households, so is the city composed of several *vici*. The second affirmation [concerns the formal characteristic of a city.] The city is the perfect community. This, ARISTOTLE explains thus: Since every communication, whenever it is found among men, is ordained to something necessary for life, that community will be the perfect community which is ordained to the end that man may have the fullness of human life: and this is the city. For it is in the city that man finds the satisfaction of whatever needs human life may have in the circumstances in which it is lived (*sicut contingit esse.*) Thus the city is composed of several *vici* in one of which the smith's craft is exercised, in another the weaver's craft, and so on. It is clear then that the city is the perfect community. In the third place, the Philosopher shows to what end or purpose the city is instituted. Its origin, indeed, may be ascribed to the purpose of simply living, inasmuch as men find in it the things which make their life livable at all. But once it exists, it will provide men with the means not only to live but also to live well, inasmuch as, by the laws of the city, life is made to be virtuous life.

[*Ibid*. 1253a 7: *The reason why man is a political animal.*]
The Philosopher demonstrates from a consideration of man's proper operation that man is a civic animal (*animal civile*), even more so than bees or other gregarious animals. This is the reason: We say that nature makes nothing in vain, because

she always works for a definite purpose. When, therefore, nature endows a being with something which, of itself, is ordained to an end, it is evident that this end is proposed to that being by nature. Now, we see that certain animals possess the faculty of making sounds, while man alone, above all other animals, has the faculty of language. Even when certain animals may utter the language of man, they do not speak in a proper sense, since they do not understand what they say but are merely trained to utter these sounds. Yet there is a difference between language and simple sound. A sound is the sign of grief and pleasure, and consequently of other passions, such as anger and fear which, as is said in the second book of the Ethics,[3] are all ordained to pleasure and grief. Therefore the faculty of sound is given to other animals, whose nature attains to the point at which they have the perceptions of pleasure and grief; and this is what they signify to one another by certain natural sounds, the lion by roaring and the dog by barking, instead of which we have our interjections. Human language, on the other hand, signifies what is advantageous and what is harmful. From this it follows that it signifies what is just and what is unjust. For justice and injustice consist in this, that several persons are adjusted, or not adjusted, to one another in respect of things advantageous or harmful. So language is proper to men, since it is a peculiarity of theirs in comparison with the rest of the animal world that they possess the knowledge of good and evil, of the just and the unjust, and of other similar relations. . . . In these things men communicate one with another naturally. Since, therefore, this communication constitutes the household and the city, man is naturally a domestic and a civic animal.

IV. *In Libros Ethicorum Aristotelis Expositio*, Lib. VIII, lect. 10 (ed. Pirotta nn. 1673-1679.)

[*Eth. Nic.* VIII, 10; 1160a 31-35: *The classification of the constitutions.*]

. . . There are three species of constitutions and an equal number of corruptions or deviation-forms. The right constitu-

---

[3]: 1104b 14.

tions are, first, *kingship*, i.e., the rule of one man; second, *aristocracy*, i.e., the rule of the best (this kind of civic order is indeed ruled by the virtuous men); thirdly, *timocracy*. Such a third species will have to be assumed, although not all agree to do so, as is said in the fifth (?) book of the *Politics*.[4] Timocracy is fittingly called so from the [Greek] word *timae* which means *remuneration* (*pretium*); for under this constitution the poor are remunerated for attending, and the rich fined for not attending, the civic assemblies, as is said in the fourth book of the *Politics*.[5] Others call this constitution by the generic name *polity*, since it is that of the rich and the poor alike; compare the fourth book of the *Politics*.[6]

[*Ibid.* 35-36: *Their respective value.*]

Comparing these constitutions the Philosopher says that the best is kingship, since under this form of government one man, and the best of all, holds power. The least good is timocracy which is the ruling of the mediocre. Between these extremes lies aristocracy in which a few of the best are ruling but with less power of action than is invested in one man acting well and possessing the plenitude of power.

[*Ibid.* 1160a 36-b 12: *On kingship and tyranny.*]

. . . Tyranny is the deviation-form or corruption of kingship. [Thus these forms stand to each other in the opposition of contrariety.] In regard to this point, ARISTOTLE shows, first, that both forms are of the same genus, for both are monarchies, i.e., one-man governments. Second, he brings out their differences, saying that they differ most widely, from which it appears that they are contraries. For contraries, being of the same genus, are most widely distant one from the other. What the difference is between tyranny and kingship, the Philosopher

---

[4] Cf. *ibid.* IV, 3: 1290a 22 (SUSEMIHL 383.)

[5] St. Thomas refers to *Pol.* V, 13: 1297a 17 ff, 20 (SUSEMIHL 428). Manifestly the translation of the word *timae* by *pretium* made it impossible for him to understand this Aristotelian teaching. The word *timocracy* is derived from *timema*, i.e., valuation of property (in Latin *census*). Timocracy thus is the rule of those who are equals, in virtue of coming up to a certain moderate property qualification. Aquinas is quite aware of the insufficiency of his commentary on timocracy, for in none of his other writings does he make use of this notion.

[6] 8: 1294a 16; 23 (SUSEMIHL 409).

declares by saying that, in this regime, the tyrant looks to his own advantage, while the king has his eye on that of his subjects. This is further evidenced in what follows: The true king, ARISTOTLE says, is sufficient for governing by his own resources and, therefore, should possess all good things: the goods of the soul, those of the body, and external goods; and he should possess them in such abundance that he be worthy and, at the same time potent, to hold power. If he is such, he needs nothing further and so will not be tempted to care for his own advantage as do those who still are in need. The king will be the benefactor of his subjects, which is the attribute of those who have an overflowing abundance of good things. If a king is not such a man, he is rather a *clerotos*, as ARISTOTLE says, which means he is king [not naturally but] by the decision of the lots. On the other hand, the tyrant, since he pursues his own interest, is the very contrary of the king. Hence it is clear that tyranny is the worst deviation-form. For it is the contrary of the best that is worst and a man passes over from kingship, *i.e.*, the best form, to tyranny which is a depravity of monarchy, *i.e.*, one-man rule; in other words, it is the bad king who becomes a tyrant. Tyranny, then, the Philosopher concludes, is the worst form of government.

[*Ibid*. 1260b 12-16: *The corruption of aristocracy.*]

. . . Aristocracy, in its turn, passes over into oligarchy, *i.e.*, the dominion of a few. This happens on account of the badness of the rulers who do not distribute according to worthiness the goods which belong to the city but snatch away either all or a great deal of them, for their own use and in order to enrich themselves and their friends. Thus it comes about that instead of the most worthy (who are the rulers in an aristocracy) there are now a few and bad man at the head of the city.

[*Ibid*. 16-22: *The corruption of timocracy.*]

. . . Timocracy, according to the Philosopher, is corrupted into democracy, *i.e.*, the power of the people. These forms are coterminous, *i.e.*, close to each other. They are alike in two regards. First, timocracy (meaning the constitution characterized by a certain system of remunerations) as well as democracy are forms of government in which the many have power; second, in either constitution the criterion of estimating who are "the best people" is the same (*omnes qui sunt in honoribus constituti sunt aequales.*) The difference between them consists in that timocracy keeps in view the common good of both the rich and the poor, while democracy knows only of the good of the poor. Hence democracy is the least bad of the deviation-forms. Its distance from timocracy which is a right constitution is very small indeed.

V. *In Libros Politicorum Aristotelis Expositio*, Lib. III, lect. 5-6.

[*Pol.* III, 6; 1279a 17-21: *The distinction between right and wrong constitutions.*]

The Philosopher propounds the distinction between right and unjust constitutions. Since dominion over free men is ordained to the interest of the subjects, it is clear that, when a constitution makes the holders of power aim at the common interest, it is a right constitution, judging by the standards of absolute justice. When, on the contrary, a constitution looks only to the interest of those who possess political power, it is a wrong constitution and a perversion of the right form. For there is, in this case, no absolute justice, *i.e.,* justice for all, but only relative justice, namely, for those who are at the top. They therefore exercise dominion over the city by using the citizens as slaves to the rulers' own advantage; and that is against justice, since the city is a community of freemen, the slaves not being citizens at all.

[*Ibid.* 7; 1279a 25-32: *The classification of the constitutions.*]

Here the Philosopher classifies the constitutions. . . . A constitution, he says, is the ordering, in a city, of those who have power and those who are subjected (*ordo dominantium in civitate.*) Therefore, the criterion for classifying the constitutions will be found in the diversity of those who possess the power. They are either One, or Few, or Many. Further, in each case, there are two different possibilities. Power is held either for the common advantage, and in this case the constitution will be right; or for the advantage of the holders themselves, and in this case the constitution will be a perversion, no matter whether power is vested in one, or a few, or many. For this is the alternative: either the subjects are not citizens: [then they have no part in the common utility]; or they [are citizens and] have their share in the common good.

[*Ibid.* 1279a 32- b 4: *The names of the right constitutions.*]
Now the Philosopher proceeds to declare the names of these constitutions. . . . If there is dominion of one man directed towards the common interest, the constitution is called *monarchy*, in the general use of language. If a few are holding the power and using it for the common good, this is an *aristocracy*, so-called because political power is held by the best, *i.e.*, the virtuous men, or again because it is used for the best interest of the city and of all citizens. Finally, if many have power and exercise it with a view to the common interest, the constitution is commonly called *polity* which is the generic name of all constitutions. There is a good reason for this usage which gives to this form the generic name. It is easy to find in a city one man or a few who are of outstanding virtue. But it is very difficult indeed for there to be many who attain to the perfection of virtue. Most likely, however, one virtue will be common to a greater number of men, *viz.*, military bravery. This is the reason why under this constitution warriors and those who carry arms are at the top.

[*Ibid.* 6-10: *The names of the perverted constitutions.*]
. . . They are as follows: The perversion of kingship is called *tyranny;* the perversion of aristocracy, *oligarchy* (which means: power of the few); finally *democracy* (meaning; power of the people, or rather the vulgar mass) is the perversion of that polity in which the many dominate but on the basis of at least one virtue, *viz.*, military bravery. Hence, ARISTOTLE concludes, tyranny is the dominion of one man aiming at his own interest; oligarchy is the dominion of a few aiming at the interest of the rich; democracy is the dominion of many aiming at the interest of the poor. None of these constitutions takes thought for the common good. . . .

[*Ibid.* 8; 1279b 34-1280a 6: *The criterion of number is not adequate.*]

[After closer examination of these definitions] it appears that, in the case of democracy the large number of the holders of power is an accidental circumstance; and likewise, in the case of oligarchy the small number is merely accidental. For it is nothing but a fact that everywhere there are more poor than rich people. The above mentioned names, therefore, owe their origin [not to a universally valid reason but] simply to a fact which happens to be true in most of the cases. Since, however, a specific differentiation cannot be obtained on the basis of what is merely accidental, it follows that, *per se,* the distinction between oligarchies and democracies cannot be made in virtue of the larger or smaller number of the rulers. Rather their specific difference results from the difference between poverty and riches. If a regime is ordained to the increase of the possessions of the rich, its very species is determined by this end and it is for this reason that it differs specifically from a regime whose end is liberty, which regime is democracy. Hence, wherever the rich hold political power, no matter whether they are many or few, there will be oligarchy; and wherever the poor hold this power, there will be democracy; and that the latter are many and the former few is nothing but an accidental circumstance. For only a few have riches yet all partake of liberty. This is why both classes fight each other. The few want to dominate for the sake of their possessions and the many want to prevail upon the few since they believe that, by the criterion of liberty, they have just as good a right to political power as the rich.

VI. *Scriptum Super Libros Sententiarum* II, *dist.* 44, q. **II, a. 2.**[7]

[The problem is whether Christians are bound to obey secular powers, especially tyrants.] The procedure in discussing this problem is this: It seems that they are not bound to this obedience. . . . The *fourth* argument [in favour of this position] runs as follows: It is legitimate for anyone, who can do so, to re-take what has been taken away from him unjustly. Now many secular princes unjustly usurped the dominion of

[7] Written around A.D. 1255.

Christian lands. Since, therefore, in such cases rebellion is legitimate, Christians have no obligation to obey these princes. —The *fifth* argument: If it is a legitimate and even a praiseworthy deed to kill a person, then no obligation of obedience exists toward that person. Now in the *Book on Duties* CICERO justifies JULIUS CAESAR's assassins.[8] Although CAESAR was a close friend of his, yet by usurping the empire he proved himself to be a tyrant. Therefore toward such powers there is no obligation of obedience.

On the other hand, however, there are the following arguments proving the contrary position: *First,* it is said: Servants, be in subjection to your masters (I *Pet.* ii, 18.) *Second,* it is also said: He that resisteth the power, withstandeth the ordinance of God (*Rom.* xiii, 2.) Now it is not legitimate to withstand the ordinance of God. Hence it is not legitimate either to withstand secular power.

Solution and determination. Obedience, by keeping a commandment, has for its [formal] object the obligation, involved in the commandment, that it be kept. Now this obligation originates in that the commanding authority has the power to impose an obligation binding not only to external but also to internal and spiritual obedience—"for conscience sake", as the Apostle says (*Rom.* xiii, 5.) For power (authority) comes from God, as the Apostle implies in the same place. Hence, Christians are bound to obey the authorities inasmuch as they are from God; and they are not bound to obey inasmuch as the authority is not from God.

Now, this not being from God may be the case, *first,* as to the mode in which authority is acquired, and, *second,* as to the use which is made of authority.

Concerning the first case we must again distinguish two defects: There may be a defect of the person acquiring authority inasmuch as this person is unworthy of it. There may also be a defect in the mode of acquiring authority, namely, if it is obtained by violence, or simony, or other illegitimate means.

As to the *first* of these defects, we say that it does not constitute an obstacle against acquiring lawful authority. Since,

[8] *De Officiis* I, 8, 26.

then, as such, authority is always from God (and this is what causes the obligation of obedience), the subjects are bound to render obedience to these authorities, unworthy as they may be.

As to the *second* of those defects, we say that in such a case there is no lawful authority at all. He who seizes power by violence does not become a true holder of power. Hence, when it is possible to do so, anybody may repel this domination, unless, of course, the usurper should later on have become a true ruler by the consent of the subjects or by a recognition being extended to him by a higher authority.

The abuse of power might take on two forms. *First*, a commandment emanating from the authority might be contrary to the very end in view of which authority is instituted, *i.e.*, to be an educator to, and a preserver of, virtue. Should therefore the authority command an act of sin contrary to virtue, we not only are not obliged to obey but we are also obliged not to obey, according to the example of the holy martyrs who preferred death to obeying those ungodly tyrants.

The *second* form of abusing power is for the authority to go beyond the bounds of its legal rights, for instance, when a master exacts duties which the servant is not bound to pay, or the like. In this case the subject is not obliged to obey, but neither is he obliged not to obey.

Consequently . . . to the *fourth* argument the answer is this: An authority acquired by violence is not a true authority, and there is no obligation of obedience, as we said above.

To the *fifth* argument the answer is that CICERO speaks of domination obtained by violence and ruse, the subjects being unwilling or even forced to accept it and there being no recourse open to a superior who might pronounce judgment upon the usurper. In this case he that kills the tyrant for the liberation of the country, is praised and rewarded.[9]

VII. *Contra Gentiles* IV, 76.

. . . It is evident that, although there are many different peoples in different dioceses and cities, yet there is one Christendom (*Populus Christianus*), just as there is one Church.'

[9]See however *Summa* II-II, 42, 2 *arg.* 3 and *ad* 3; *ibid.* 64, 3.

Therefore, just as there is one bishop appointed to one particular people in order to be the head of them all, so in the whole of Christendom one must be the head of the whole Church. . . .

JOHN OF PARIS[10] *thought fit to correct this text in the following way*: It is evident that, although there are many different peoples in different dioceses and cities, in which the bishops hold authority in matters spiritual, yet there is one Church of all the Faithful and one Christendom. Therefore, just as there is one bishop in every diocese appointed to be the head of the particular church of that people, so in the whole Church and in the whole of Christendom, there is one supreme bishop, *viz.*, the Pope.

VIII. *Scriptum Super Libros Sententiarum* II, dist. 44, *Expositio textus*.

[The problem is whether we should obey a superior authority more than an inferior one.] If the position be taken that such is indeed our duty, this seems not to be true. . . . For [*fourth* argument] spiritual power is higher than secular power. If, then, it were true that we must obey more the superior power, the spiritual power would have the right always to release a man from his allegiance to a secular power, which is evidently not true.

Solution and determination. Two cases are to be considered in which we find the superior and the inferior authorities standing in different relations one to the other. *First,* the inferior authority originates totally from the superior authority. In this case, absolutely speaking and in all events, greater obedience is due to the superior power. An illustration of this is the order of natural causes: the first cause has a stronger impact upon the thing caused by a second cause than has this very second cause, as is said in the *Liber De Causis*.[11] In this position we find God's power in regard to every created power, or likewise the Emperor's power in regard to that of the Proconsul, or again the Pope's power in regard to every

---

[10]*De Potestate Regia et Papali* (A.D. 1302), ch. III, ed. LECLERCQ 180.
[11]First proposition; see St. Thomas' *Expos.* 1 (193, 196).

spiritual power in the Church, since by the Pope all degrees of different dignities in the Church are distributed and ordered. Whence papal authority is one of the foundations of the Church, as is evident from *Matth.* xvi, 18. So in all things, without any distinction, the Pope ought to be obeyed more than Bishops and Archbishops; (more also by the monk than is the abbot.) — The *second* case to be considered is, that both the superior and the inferior powers originate from one supreme power. Their subordination, thus, depends on the latter who subordinates one to the other as he pleases. As to this case we say that here one power is superior to the other only in regard to those matters in view of which they have been so subordinated one to the other by that supreme power. Hence in these matters alone greater obedience is due to the superior than to the inferior. An example of this is our relation to the authorities of a Bishop and an Archbishop, both of which descend from the papal authority.

The answer then . . . to the *fourth* argument is this. Spiritual as well as secular power comes from the divine power. Hence secular power is subjected to spiritual power in those matters concerning which the subjection has been specified and ordained by God, *i.e.*, in matters belonging to the salvation of the soul. Hence in these we are to obey spiritual authority more than secular authority. On the other hand, more obedience is due to secular than to spiritual power in the things that belong to the civic good (*bonum civile*). For it is said *Matth.* xxii, 21: Render unto Caesar the things that are Caesar's. A special case occurs, however, when spiritual and secular power are so joined in one person as they are in the Pope, who holds the apex of both spiritual and secular powers. This has been so arranged by Him who is both Priest and King, *Priest Eternal after the order of Melchisedech, King of Kings and Lord of Lords, Whose dominion shall not pass away, and his kingdom shall not be destroyed for ever and ever. Amen.*[12]

[12]This passage concludes the second book of the *Scriptum;* this explains the doxological ending.

LIST OF BOOKS USED

ALBERT THE GREAT, ST., *Liber de natura locorum. B. Alberti Magni Opera omnia*, ed. Auguste Borgnet, vol. IX, pp. 528-582. Paris, 1890.

—— *De more et vita. Ibid.*, pp. 346-371.

ALFRED OF SARESHEL, *Des Alfred von Sareshel (Alfredus Anglicus) Schrift "De motu cordis."* Hrsg. von Clemens Baeumker. *Beiträge zur Geschichte der Philosophie und Theologie des Mittelalters* XXIII, 1-2. Münster i. W., 1923.

AMBROSIASTER, THE, *Quaestiones Veteris et Novi Testamenti* (Pseudo-Augustine). Migne, *PL* vol. 35, 2215-2422.

ARISTOTLE. *Aristoteles graece, ex recensione Immanuelis Bekkeri.* Ed. *Academia Regia Borussica.* 2 vols. Berlin, 1831.

—— *Aristotelis Politicorum libri octo cum vetusta translatione Guilelmi de Moerbeka.* Ed. F. Susemihl. Leipzig, 1872.

—— *The Politics of Aristotle.* Ed. W. L. Newman. 4 vols. Oxford, 1887-1902.

—— *The Works of Aristotle.* Transl. under the editorship of W. D. Ross. 11 vols. Oxford, 1908-1931.

—— *The Politics of Aristotle.* Transl. by Ernest Barker. Oxford, 1947.

AUGUSTINE, ST., *De civitate Dei libri XXII.* Ed. Bernhard Dombart. Third ed. 2 vols. Leipzig, 1909.

—— *De libero arbitrio.* Migne, *PL* vol. 32, 1221-1310.

AVICENNA, *De anima (Sextus naturalium).* In *Auicenne perhypatetici philosophi . . . opera.* Venice, 1508.

BARKER, ERNEST: see ARISTOTLE.

BARTOLUS DE SAXOFERRATO (Sassoferrato), *Consilia, Quaestiones et Tractatus.* Turin, 1589.

LIST OF BOOKS REFERRED TO 109

BERGES, W., *Die Fürstenspiegel des hohen und späten Mittelalters. Schriften des Reichsinstituts für ältere deutsche Geschichtskunde*, II. Leipzig, 1938.

BROWNE, MICHAEL, O.P., *An sit authenticum opusculum s. Thomae "De regimine principum."* In *Angelicum* III, pp. 300-303. Rome, 1926.

CAESAR, C. *Iulii Caesaris Commentarii belli gallici.* Leipzig, 1927.

Cambridge Mediaeval History. Vol. VI. Cambridge, 1929.

CARLYLE, R. W. and A. J., *A History of Mediaeval Political Theory in the West.* 6 vols. Edinburgh, 1903-1936.

Chartularium Universitatis Parisiensis, ed. Denifle-Chatelain. 4 vols. Paris, 1889-1897.

CHENU, M.-C., O.P., (Book reviews in) *Bulletin thomiste* I ff. Bellevue (S.-et-O.); Juvisy (S.-et-O.), 1924 ff.

CICERO. M. *Tulli Ciceronis Scripta quae manserunt omnia.* Leipzig, 1914-1933.

COBHAM, C. D., *Excerpta Cypria. Materials for a History of Cyprus.* Cambridge, 1908.

DELABORDE, H.-F., *Lettre des Chrétiens de Terre-Sainte à Charles d'Anjou* (22 avril 1260). In *Revue de l'Orient latin* II, 206-215. Paris, 1894.

DENIFLE, HEINRICH, O.P., *Quellen zur Gelehrtengeschichte des Predigerordens im 13. und 14. Jahrh.* In *Archiv für Litteratur und Kirchengeschichte des Mittelalters* II, pp. 165-248. Berlin, 1886.

DE RUBEIS, BERNARD, O.P., *De gestis et scriptis ac doctrina s. Thomae Aquinatis dissertationes criticae et apologeticae* (A.D. 1750.) In *S. Thomae Opera omnia* (Ed. Leonina), vol. I, pp. XLV-CCCXLVI. Rome, 1882.

DIONYSIUS (the Pseudo-Areopagite), *De caelesti hierarchia.* Migne, *PG* vol 3, 119-370.

——— *De divinis nominibus. Ibid.*, 585-984.

DONDAINE, A., O.P., *Guillaume Peyraut, vie et oeuvres.* In *Archivum Fratrum Praedicatorum* XVIII, pp. 162-236. Rome, 1948.

ECHARD, JACQUES, See QUETIF, JACQUES.

110 ON KINGSHIP

110　　ON KINGSHIP

EGIDIUS ROMANUS, *De regimine principum*. Rome, 1482.

ENDRES, J. A., *De regimine principum des hl. Thomas von Aquin.* Beiträge zur Geschichte der Philosophie und Theologie des Mittelalters, Supplementband, Festgabe Clemens Baeumker, pp. 261-267. Münster i. W., 1913.

ESCHMANN, I. TH., O.P., *A Thomistic Glossary on the Principle of the Preeminence of a Common Good.* In *Mediaeval Studies* V, pp. 123-165. Toronto, 1943.

EUSEBIUS PAMPHILUS, *Chronicorum libri duo.* Migne *PG* vol. 19, 99-598.

FLORI, EZIO, *Il trattato "De regimine principum."* Bologna, 1927.

FRETTE, S.-E. See THOMAS AQUINAS, ST.

GARRISON, F. H., *An Introduction to the History of Medicine.* Second ed. Philadelphia and London, 1917.

GELASIUS, ST., *Tomus.* Migne, *PL* vol. 59, 102-110.

GIERKE, OTTO, *Political Theories of the Middle Ages.* Transl. by F. W. Maitland. Cambridge, 1913.

GILSON, ETIENNE, *La philosophie au moyen âge.* Third ed. Paris, 1947.

───── *Le thomisme. Introduction à la philosophie de s. Thomas.* Fifth ed. Paris, 1944.

───── *Dante the Philosopher.* Transl. by David Moore. London, 1948.

GLORIEX, PALEMON, *Pour la chronologie de la Somme de s. Thomas d'Aquin.* In *Mélanges de science religieuse* II, pp. 59-98. Lille, 1945.

Glossa ordinaria in evangelium secundum Matthaeum. Migne, *PL* vol. 114, 63-178.

GOODENOUGH, E. R., *The Political Philosophy of Hellenistic Kingship.* In *Yale Classical Studies,* vol. I, pp. 55-102. New Haven, 1928.

GRABMANN, MARTIN, *Die Werke des hl. Thomas von Aquin.* Beiträge zur Geschichte der Philosophie und Theologie des Mittelalters XXII, 1-2. Münster i. W., 1931.

───── *Studien über den Einfluss der aristotelischen Philosophie auf die mittelalterlichen Theorien über das Verhältnis von Kirche und Staat. Sitzungsberichte der bayerischen Akademie der Wissenschaften, Phil.-hist. Abtlg, 1934, 2.* München, 1934.

—— *Guglielmo di Moerbeke O.P., il traduttore delle opere di Aristotele. Miscellanea historiae Pontificiae,* vol. XI. Rome, 1946.

—— *Mittelalterliches Geistesleben* II, München, 1936.

GRANDCLAUDE, M., *Les particularités du De regimine principum. Communication aux journées d'histoire du droit.* In *Revue historique du droit français et étranger* VIII, p. 665 f. Paris, 1929.

GRATIAN. *Decretum Magistri Gratiani. Corpus iuris canonici* I. Ed. by Aem. Friedberg. Leipzig, 1879.

GREGORY I., ST., *Moralium libri.* Migne, PL vol. 75, 509-1162; 76, 9-782.

—— *XL homiliarum in evangelia libri duo.* Migne, PL vol. 76, 1075-1312.

—— *Regulae pastoralis liber.* Migne, PL vol. 77, 12-128.

GREGORY IX. *Decretalium Gregorii IX collectio. Corpus iuris canonici II.* Ed Aem. Friedberg. Leipzig, 1881.

GROUSSET, RENE, *Histoire de l'Orient latin.* In Charles Diehl, etc., *Histoire du moyen âge* IX, 1, pp. 436-591. Paris, 1945.

GUIBERT DE TOURNAI, *Le traité Eruditio regum et principum de Guibert de Tournai, O. F. M.* Ed. A. De Poorter. *Les philosophes belges,* vol. IX. Louvain, 1914.

HILL, SIR G. F., *A History of Cyprus.* Vol. II: *The Frankish Period.* Cambridge, 1948.

ISIDORE, ST. *Isidori Hispalensis Episcopi Etymologiarum libri XX.* Ed. W. M. Lindsay. 2 vols. Oxford, 1911.

—— *Sententiarum libri tres.* Migne, PL vol. 83, 537-738.

JEROME, ST. *S. Eusebii Hieronymi De viris illustribus liber.* Migne, PL vol. 23, 631-760.

JOHN OF PARIS, *De potestate regia et papali.* Ed. J. Leclercq, *Jean de Paris et l'ecclésiologie du XIIIe siècle,* pp. 171-260. Paris, 1942.

JOHN OF SALISBURY. *Ioannis Saresberiensis Policratici libri VIII.* Ed. C. C. I. Webb. 2 vols. Oxford, 1909.

JOSEPHUS, FLAVIUS, Ed. and transl. by H. St. J. Thackeray and Ralph Marcus. *The Loeb Classical Library.* 7 vols. Cambridge (Mass.), 1926-1943.

JOURDAIN, CHARLES, *La philosophie de s. Thomas d'Aquin.* Vol. I. Paris, 1858.

112   ON KINGSHIP

JOURNET, CHARLES. See THOMAS AQUINAS, ST.

KIMBLE, H. T., *Geography in the Middle Ages*. London, 1938.

LEHMANN, PAUL, *Mittelalterliche Bibliothekskataloge Deutsch-lands und der Schweiz*. Vol. II, *Bistum Mainz, Erfurt*. München, 1928.

LIVY, *Ab Urbe condita*. Ed. Conway-Walters. 4 vols. Oxford, 1914-1934.

MANDONNET, PIERRE, O.P., *Des écrits authentiques de s. Thomas d'Aquin*. 2nd ed. Fribourg (Suisse), 1910.

―――― and DESTREZ, JEAN, *Bibliographie thomiste*. *Biblio-thèque thomiste* vol. I. Le Saulchoir (Kain), 1921.

―――― *Les opuscules de s. Thomas d'Aquin*. Introduction to the ed. of *Opuscula omnia*, vol. I. Paris, 1927.

MANEGOLD OF LAUTENBACH. *Manegoldi ad Gebehardum liber*. Ed. K. Franke. In *Monumenta Germaniae historica, Libelli de lite* I, pp. 300-430. Hannover, 1891.

MARIANI, U., O.S.A., *Scrittori politici agostiniani del sec. XIV*. Firenze, 1927.

MAS LATRIE, LOUIS DE, *Histoire de l'Ile de Chypre sous le règne de la Maison de Lusignan*. 3 vols. Paris, 1861, 1852/3.

McILWAIN, C. H., *The Growth of Political Thought in the West*. New York, 1932.

MEERSSEMAN, GILLES, O.P., *Laurentii Pignon Catalogi et Chronica*. *Monumenta Ordinis Fratrum Praedicatorum historica*, vol. XVIII. Rome, 1936.

MENKO. *Menkonis Chronicon*. Ed. Ludwig Weiland. In *Monumenta Germ. Hist. Scriptores* XXIII, 523-561. Hannover, 1874.

MULLER-THYM, B. J., *The Establishment of the University of Being in the Doctrine of Meister Eckhart*. New York, 1939.

NEWMAN, W. L. See ARISTOTLE.

O'BRIEN, G. A. T., *An Essay on Mediaeval Economic Teaching*. London, 1920.

O'RAHILLY, ALFRED, *Notes on St. Thomas. IV. De Regimine Principum; V. Tolomeo of Lucca, the Continuator of the 'De Regimine Principum'*. In *Irish Ecclesiastical Record*. Fifth Series, XXXI, pp. 396-410; 606-614. Dublin, 1928.

PETER COMESTOR, *Historia scholastica*. Migne, *PL* vol. 198, 1053-1721.

PHELAN, G. B. See THOMAS AQUINAS, ST.

PIRENNE, HENRI, *Medieval Cities*. Transl. by F. D. Halsey. Princeton, 1925.

PSEUDO-ARISTOTLE, *Secretum Secretorum*. Ed Robert Steele in *Opera hactenus inedita Rogeri Baconi*, fasc. V., pp. 1-172. Oxford, 1920.

QUETIF, JACQUES, O.P., and ECHARD, JACQUES, O.P., *Scriptores Ordinis Praedicatorum*. 2 vols. Paris, 1719.

ROGUET, CLAUDE. See THOMAS AQUINAS, ST.

SALLUST, Ed. and transl. by J. C. Rolfe. *The Loeb Classical Library*. London, 1921.

SCHMEIDLER, BERNHARD, *Die Annalen des Tholomeus von Lucca*. *Monumenta Germaniae Historica, Script.*, Nova series VIII. Berlin, 1930.

Scriptores Ord. Praed. See QUETIF, JACQUES.

SENECA, L. *Annaei Senecae Opera quae supersunt*. Leipzig, 1905-1914.

SIMONIN, H.-D., O.P., *Notes de bibliographie dominicaine*. In *Archivum Fr. Praed.* VIII, 193-214; IX, 192-213. Rome, 1938-1939.

STEELE, ROBERT. See PSEUDO-ARISTOTLE.

STOBAEUS, *Ioannis Stobaei Anthologium*. Ed. C. Wachsmuth, O. Hense. 4 vols. Berlin, 1884-1912.

STUBBS, WILLIAM, *Seventeen Lectures on the Study of Mediaeval and Modern History*. 3rd ed.. Oxford, 1900.

SUETONIUS. Ed. and transl. by J. C. Rolfe. *The Loeb Classical Library*. 2 vols. London, 1928, 1930.

SUSEMIHL, F. See ARISTOTLE.

SYNAVE, P., O.P., *Le Catalogue Officiel des oeuvres de s. Thomas d'Aquin*. In *Archives d'histoire doctrinale et littéraire du moyen âge* III, pp. 25-103. Paris, 1928.

THOMAS AQUINAS, ST.

Sent. = *Scriptum super libros Sententiarum*. Ed. Vivès, *Opera omnia* VII-X. Paris, 1873.

CG = *Summa contra gentiles*. Editio Leonina manualis. Rome, 1934.

Summa = *Summa theologiae*. Ed. Inst. Stud. Med. Ottav. 4 vols. Ottawa, 1941-1944.

In Eth. = *In Libros Ethicorum expositio*. Ed. Angelo Pirotta. Turin, 1934.

In Pol. = *In libros Politicorum expositio.* Ed Vivès, *Opera omnia* XXVI, 89-226. Paris, 1875.

In Met. = *In Libros Metaphysicorum expositio.* Ed. M. R. Cathala. Turin, 1926.

In De An. = *In libros De anima expositio.* Ed. Angelo Pirotta. Turin, 1925.

De Pot. = *Quaestio disputata De potentia.* Turin, 1931.

Quodl. = *Quaestiones quodlibetales.* Turin, 1927.

Catena Aurea in quatuor Evangelia. 2 vols. Turin, 1925.

In Matth. = *In Evangelium Matthaei lectura. In Evangelia commentaria,* I. Ed. Taurinensis IV. Turin, 1925.

In Ioan. = *In Evangelium Ioannis lectura. In Evangelia commentaria,* II. Ed. cit.

In omnes S. Pauli Epistolas commentaria. Ed. Taurinensis VII. 2 vols. Turin, 1929.

De causis = *In librum De causis expositio. Opuscula omnia.* Ed. Mandonnet I, 193-311.

Expositio super Dionysium De divinis nominibus. Ibid. II, 220-654.

C. Imp. = *Contra impugnantes Dei cultum et religionem. Ibid.* IV, 1-195.

De Perf. = *De perfectione vitae spiritualis. Ibid.* IV, 196-264.

Contra errores Graecorum. Ibid. III, 279-327.

Du gouvernement royal. (French) transl. by Claude Roguet. Preface by Charles Journet. Paris, 1931.

On the Governance of Rulers. Transl. by G. B. Phelan. Toronto, 1935.

De rege et regno, ad regem Cypri. Ed. by S.-E. Fretté, *In Opera omnia* XXVII. Paris, 1875.

THORNDIKE, LYNN and KIBRE, PEARL, *A Catalogue of Incipits of Mediaeval Scientific Writings in Latin.* Cambridge (Mass.), 1937.

TOLOMEO OF LUCCA, *De Regimine principum.* Ed. Mandonnet. In *St. Thomas, Opuscula omnia* I, pp. 353 (?) - 487. Paris, 1927.

UCCELLI, P. A., *Intorno a' due opuscoli di S. Tommaso d'Aquino sul governo de' sudditi al re di Cipro ed alla duchessa di Fiandra.* In *La scienza e la fede* LXXVI, 106-125. Naples, 1870 (Offprint).

LIST OF BOOKS REFERRED TO 115

VALERIUS MAXIMUS, *Valerii Maximi Factorum et dictorum memorabilium libri IX.* Leipzig, 1888.

VEGETIUS, *Flavi Vegeti Renati Epitoma rei militaris.* Ed. C. Lang. Leipzig, 1885.

VINCENT OF BEAUVAIS. *Speculum historiale Vincentii . . . Bellovacensis.* Venice, 1494.

—— *Speculum doctrinale. . . .* Venice, 1494.

—— *De eruditione filiorum nobilium.* Ed. Arpad Steiner. Cambridge (Mass.), 1938.

VITRUVIUS, *On Architecture.* Ed. and transl. by F. S. Granger. The Loeb Classical Library. 2 vols. London, 1931-1934.

WALZ, ANGELO, O.P., *San Tommaso d'Aquino.* Rome, 1945.

WENDLAND, PAUL, *Die hellenistisch-römische Kultur.* Tübingen, 1912.

INDEX OF NAMES